washington's
RAIL-TRAILS

washington's
RAIL-TRAILS

Walking
Running
Bicycling
In-line Skating
Horseback Riding

second edition

FRED WERT

THE
MOUNTAINEERS
BOOKS

Published by
The Mountaineers Books
1001 SW Klickitat Way, Suite 201
Seattle, WA 98134

First edition 1992, second edition, 2001

Published simultaneously in Great Britain by Cordee, 3a DeMontfort Street, Leicester, England, LE1 7HD

Manufactured in the United States of America

Project Editor: Kathleen Cubley
Editor: Carol Anne Peschke
Cover design, book design, and layout: Kristy L. Welch
Mapmakers: Fred Wert and Mayumi Thompson

Unless otherwise noted, all photographs are by the author.

Cover photograph: *Columbia Plateau Trail* © Fred Wert
Frontispiece: *Milwaukee Road Corridor Trail* © Fred Wert

Library of Congress Cataloging-in-Publication Data

Wert, Fred, 1949-
  Washington's rail-trails : walking, running, bicycling, in-line
skating, horseback riding / Fred Wert.— 2nd ed.
      p. cm.
Includes indexes.
  ISBN 0-89886-776-2
  1. Rail-trails—Washington (State)—Guidebooks. 2. Outdoor
recreation—Washington (State)—Guidebooks. 3. Washington
(State)—Guidebooks. I. Title.
  GV191.42.W2 W48 2001
  796.5'09797—dc21
                                              00-012826

contents

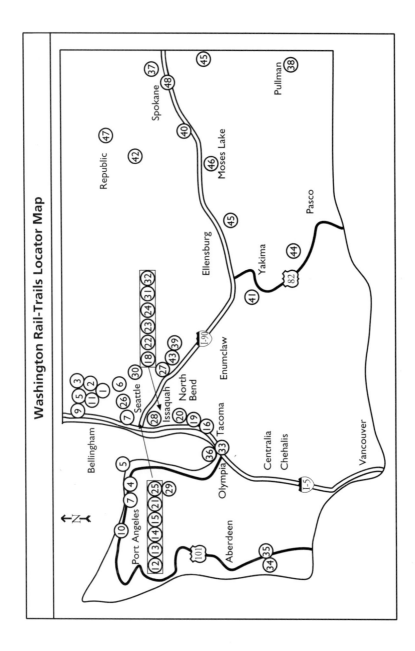

Washington Rail-Trails Locator Map

preface

An important part of Washington's history is quietly disappearing. As the result of economic pressures, many railroad lines are being abandoned throughout the state. Railroads were the first major transportation system developed in Washington, and they were critical for its economic development. Ironically, economics is slowly eroding their importance as a transportation system today.

Thousands of miles of railroads were built throughout Washington, from main-line routes to short logging lines that existed just long enough to get the trees out. The construction of these railroads significantly altered the shape of the land by making narrow, flat strips of railway roadbed. When the railroad companies leave, they take with them the rails, ties, and trains. But the railroad beds—the graded dirt and gravel, the long narrow strips of smooth land—remain. Looking closely, one can see these abandoned rights-of-way everywhere: along rivers and streams, in second-growth forests, behind urban warehouses, in the routing of country roads, and concealed under freeways. Some people view these corridors as scars on the land. But more and more people are seeing them as an opportunity to create rail-trails: public-access trails built on abandoned railroad rights-of-way.

Rail-trails serve many public needs. They provide recreational opportunities for a wide range of nonmotorized uses, more than any other kind of trail. They preserve unique greenspace, contributing to the green aesthetic that is so much a part of the natural beauty of Washington State. They also keep alive the last vestiges of railroad history in a more visible and active way than the few remaining steam engines displayed at local parks. Rail-trails provide a connection between public parks and open space in a way roads can never achieve. And they may well serve future needs as public corridors for high-speed rail or, if oil reserves are depleted, low-speed nonmotorized use.

There is a sense of urgency in developing rail-trails. Once a railroad abandons operations, the land can revert to many owners, and it may be very difficult to reassemble the same corridor of land from numerous small parcels. The result can be very daunting to government agencies, even if they have an interest in the rail-trail concept.

It is the goal of this book to increase public awareness of existing rail-trails, their singular and wonderful qualities, and the opportunities for further rail-trail development in Washington State. Timing is critical, and it is hoped that this book will help citizens realize what a valuable resource rail-trails are and ensure the continued development of all potential rail-trails. Now is the time for citizens and public officials to take action, or this unique resource will be lost forever.

Fred Wert, Winthrop, 2000

introduction

Throughout Washington abandoned railroad rights-of-way are being converted to nonmotorized trails for public recreation. These rail-trails are a valuable addition to the public trails of this state. They are linear parks, publicly accessible corridors that preserve open space, provide wildlife habitat, and serve as a valuable recreational resource. When most people think of trails they think of mountain trails that are steep, narrow, and rugged. Rail-trails are different. They are wide, have very gentle grades, and occur generally in lowland areas near cities and water.

A rail-trail is a public access trail constructed on an abandoned railroad right-of-way or adjacent to an existing railroad. Its condition can vary from a rugged, overgrown dirt path to 12-foot-wide pavement with restrooms, benches, trailheads, and viewpoints. Converting these abandoned railroad rights-of-way into rail-trails provides wonderful and unique opportunities for walking, running, wheelchair use, bicycling, horseback riding, and many other human-powered activities. Their special features make them ideal as multiple-use trails.

Washington State has been a pioneer in developing rail-trails. The Burke–Gilman Trail and the King County Interurban Trail both opened in the early 1970s, and now there are more than fifty rail-trails in the state. Washington also has one of the nation's longest rail-trails. The combination of Iron Horse State Park and the Milwaukee Road Corridor Trail stretches more than 200 miles across the state, from Cedar Falls near North Bend to the Idaho border.

Rail-trails are being developed throughout the nation at an accelerating pace as railway companies continue to abandon rights-of-way and citizen action groups seize the opportunity to create rail-trails. There are about 1000 rail-trails nationwide, covering more than 10,000 miles, with many more rail-trails planned for development in the next few years.

Rail-trails vary in their location, from cities to lowland forests, from wide, paved surfaces to rough rock ballast, from urban connectors to scenic vistas. They generally traverse lowland areas that are usually snow-free in winter, unlike most backcountry trails. They are also efficient bicycle routes, safe places to walk horses and pull horse-drawn wagons, and gentle winter recreation areas.

UNIQUE FEATURES OF RAIL-TRAILS

Rail-trails are not like most other trails. They have many characteristics that make them unique:

▮ The route already exists. A converted railroad grade provides an established, feasible route. This saves much time and money for the trail's managing agency. One of the primary reasons most rail-trails in this book exist is because the abandoned railroad grade provided a ready-made and obvious trail.

▮ The trail is already built. Because the departing railway company usually has removed the rails and ties, the remaining rail bed is immediately usable as a trail. Sometimes the surface is modified by the addition of smaller gravel or paving, but essentially the trail is ready for use. This is distinctly different from trying to carve a trail through the woods or over and under roads in urban areas.

▮ Rail-trails have gentle grades. Railroads were built at minimum inclines, with most main-line grades never exceeding a 2.2 percent grade and logging railroads seldom exceeding 4 percent. Compared with many backcountry trails, rail-trails are flat and smooth, with very gentle grades.

▮ They provide excellent nonmotorized transportation routes. Communities were built around railroad lines, and when railroad rights-of-way are turned into rail-trails, they connect the communities. In King County, the Burke–Gilman Trail and the King County Interurban Trail are both excellent examples of routes used by people commuting by bicycle or foot to work.

▮ They can provide revenue for operating agencies. Several trail agencies have contracts with telecommunications companies that place their fiberoptic lines underground on rail-trails. This provides income for parks departments that can be used to maintain and operate rail-trails. The Iron Horse State Park has two long-distance fiberoptic lines buried beneath it, providing revenue to the Washington State Parks and Recreation Commission.

▮ They provide recreational opportunities for special-needs trail users. Older adults and those with disabilities, small children riding bicycles, babies in baby carriages, people who use wheelchairs, and horse-drawn wagons all need a wide path with a gentle grade. Rail-trails can provide a safe, easy path for a variety of special-needs trail users.

▮ They can provide access roads for utility corridors. Many railroad routes are used by electric utilities for voltage transmission lines. Rail-trails can offer improved access to these lines using standard utility trucks.

▮ They can serve as dikes along rivers and oceans. Because railroads needed gentle grades, many were built near rivers and streams, following the gentle grades of natural waterways.

▮ They preserve historic structures. As part of the development of rail-trails, many old railway structures are being preserved, especially old railway stations. There are also several significant railroad trestles and other structures in Washington that are protected by the State Historic Preservation Act. In addition, the railroad grades themselves are considered historic sites.

Railroad Bikeway, Bellingham

▮ They provide economic opportunities for some towns. People who use rail-trails do so primarily for recreation and are willing to travel to good recreation spots. Trail users buy gas, food, and lodging and visit small towns such as Tekoa, Waterville, Washtunca, Benge, and Pe Ell.

▮ They preserve wildlife habitat. The 50- to 200-foot-wide corridors owned by railroads often have not been disturbed for several decades and in some places are the only undeveloped land. This land provides wildlife habitat that might not otherwise exist. A good example of this is the King County Interurban Trail, which is surrounded by warehouses but also includes wetlands supporting many mammals, reptiles, birds, and insects.

▮ They provide numerous access points. Many long-distance backcountry mountain trails have few access points. Rail-trails are located primarily in lowland areas, and population centers were built up around them. Often they have many access points where a public road crosses them, and thus it is easy to use just part of the entire trail length.

The many unique features of rail-trails are only now being discovered by trail managers and trail users. The development of a system of rail-trails throughout Washington may well make them the state's most popular trails in the future.

RAILROAD HISTORY

Railroads were the first major transportation systems across the nation and around the state. They served as the first reliable high-speed transportation service for both freight and people and were an important reason for Washington's rapid growth at the turn of the century. Many railroads were built specifically for logging or mining, the remnants of which can still be seen by the careful observer.

At one time there were more than 5000 miles of interstate railroad lines in Washington, with several more thousand miles of logging and mining railroads. With the increased use of trucks, some railroad lines have gradually become uneconomical. It is less expensive and more flexible to haul for short distances and move lightweight goods by truck. Consequently, since 1970 more than 2000 miles of railroads have been abandoned in Washington State, with many more miles likely to be abandoned in the next few years.

Railroads left their mark on the landscape as many cities and towns were built alongside the tracks. Many communities were deserted long ago, and all signs of civilization disappeared except for the railway grades. Some of the place names mentioned in this book are those of old railroad stations and may not show up on modern maps, especially state highway maps. Several rail-trails are named for the original railroads. The Spruce Railroad Trail was named after the railway built during World War II to harvest valuable stands of spruce on the Olympic Peninsula. The Milwaukee Road Corridor Trail was named after the common name for the Chicago, Milwaukee, St. Paul, and Pacific Railroad.

This book does not try to document every trail that exists on a railroad right-of-way in Washington. There are thousands of miles of abandoned logging railroads; many of these are now motor vehicle roads, and some are parts of hiking trails. This book concentrates on rail-trails built primarily on main-line or interstate commerce railroad rights-of-way and on those where there has been significant historical trail development. It also limits rail-trails to those that are generally open to all types of users.

HOW RAIL-TRAILS ARE CREATED

Citizen action groups create rail-trails when they see the opportunity to turn an abandoned railway grade into a nonmotorized path. The public often is first aware that a railroad is being abandoned when the rails and ties are removed. This is also the time when most people consider using the abandoned right-of-way for trail purposes. To embark on the conversion procedure it is critical to have a thorough understanding of the abandonment process.

Why Railroads Are Abandoned

The Surface Transportation Board (STB), formerly the Interstate Commerce Commission (ICC), regulates all main-line railroads that conduct interstate commerce. The STB controls not only the operation of active lines but also their abandonment. Because the railroads that serve shippers have a monopoly on the rail business along a specific line, the STB tries to ensure that railroads do not charge excessive rates or close down a line without notice. The theory is that they serve a public good in providing rail service.

The economics of transportation have changed greatly from the days when railroads were being built. At the turn of the century there were very few roads and no trucks. Now there is strong competition from truck and water transport. The result is less railroad traffic, and some lines are becoming less profitable. When a railroad decides that it is losing money on a particular section of track, it can file a formal legal request to the STB to seek permission to stop providing service and abandon that section of track. The STB normally approves such requests without a hearing unless comments or complaints are filed by shippers on the line to be abandoned or by other interested parties.

Rail-Banking

The 1983 National Trails Act added another alternative to abandoning a railroad line. This act makes it possible for organizations to rail-bank a railroad line instead of allowing it to be abandoned. When the STB declares a line abandoned, this means that the railroad can stop serving shippers, discontinue tariffs, and pull up the rails and ties. It also means that any easements the railroad has to use other parties' lands for railroad purposes terminate. A railroad easement is a legal interest (like a lease) for use of a piece of land contingent on the land being used for railroad purposes. If a railroad ceases operations, its interest in the land returns to the holder of the easement, usually the heirs of the original easement with the railroad but sometimes also the current adjacent landowner.

Rail-banking does not include legal abandonment of the line. The STB allows the railroad to discontinue tariffs, remove rails and ties, and sell the land that the railroad owns. The purchaser of the land under rail-banking has to agree that in the future, should a railroad company want to use the line for railroad purposes, the purchaser will sell back the land for railroad purposes. The interim property owner also must agree that the right-of-way will be used for trail purposes.

Rail-banking is a powerful tool for government agencies planning to acquire a railroad right-of-way for a trail. This is because the agency can acquire all the land the railroad is using without any land reverting to adjacent property owners who have an underlying interest. The alternative, necessary if the railroad abandons the line, is to purchase individual parcels of land from many individual landowners, a very difficult and expensive undertaking.

Developing Rail-Trails

The development of rail-trails is different from the development of other public park or recreation facility projects. Most often only a few people know in advance that a railroad is going to remove the rails and ties and abandon a line. Once this has happened, it may be too late to begin converting this railroad right-of-way to a pathway through the city or the country.

The first and often most difficult step is to acquire the railroad right-of-way. As mentioned earlier, it is critical for the potential rail-trail developer to be ready before the railroad applies to the STB for abandonment so that the agency can request rail-banking. Part of this preparation is to have public support for the project and the trail route in the agency's planning documents. The agency should also ask to be notified by the railroad of any pending abandonment.

Columbia Plateau Trail

Agency Plans

Most rail-trails in Washington State are built by public agencies. These agencies provide public facilities for citizens and are usually stable, continuing entities. Usually it is the local parks departments that get involved in developing rail-trails, although public works departments may also play a part. An important aspect of any agency's work is to prepare planning documents, especially for new or expanded capital projects. These documents require the approval of elected officials and are the roadmap and authority for agency staff to proceed. They are also important for gaining public input and for applying for funding to the Washington State's Inter-Agency Committee for Outdoor Recreation (IAC).

Trail Funding

Funding is a major challenge in developing rail-trails. The first requirement is acquisition funds. The cost of acquiring a railroad right-of-way varies widely, depending on whether the railroad property is located in an urban area or on marginal land, for example. The cost for many projects amounts to several hundred thousand dollars, which is higher than the cost of many park acquisition projects.

Another funding problem arises from the fact that rail-trails are a new type of park project. Many park department directors get a tremendous amount of pressure from the public—from very well-organized and vocal groups—for more baseball, soccer, golf, and tennis facilities. Also, there is no history of rail-trail development for many city, county, or state agencies to consult for guidance.

However, there are funding opportunities for rail-trails other than the traditional sources available for parks and recreation facilities. Because they are linear and continuous, rail-trails make excellent sites for a variety of utilities. Often utilities find acquiring a continuous corridor of land far less expensive than trying to create a new corridor. Installing power lines, fiberoptic cables, water lines, and sewers is perfectly compatible with rail-trail development. In some cases, utility companies buy the land and prepare the trail surfaces as part of their use of the land.

The Washington Wildlife and Recreation Coalition has created a new source of funding. This nonprofit, statewide organization was formed solely to get legislative approval of millions of dollars to acquire and develop wildlife and recreation land throughout the state. A portion of this funding is reserved for trails. As important as trails are to the people of Washington, this is the first time there has been a dedicated funding source for trails, and it is a viable source for rail-trail funding. This funding is available through the Washington Wildlife and Recreation Program of the IAC.

Trail Design

Once a right-of-way has been acquired, the next step is to design the rail-trail and decide what type of improvements will be made. This process sometimes includes a master plan of the entire project that identifies the route, trailhead sites, and the trail surface design. An important part of the design phase is developing a trail management plan. This plan considers all the concerns of the trail manager, adjacent property owners, trail users, and emergency services personnel.

Seattle Waterfront Path

Trail Construction

The last major phase of rail-trail development is construction. This is usually a straightforward process. Often it is easier to get acquisition funds than construction funds. One alternative for the trail manager is to involve user groups that are willing to volunteer to help in construction, thus reducing costs and opening a rail-trail to the public more quickly. Several user groups have been active in trail construction in Washington State, including the Backcountry Horsemen of Washington, The Mountaineers, Volunteers for Outdoor Washington, and the Backcountry Bicycle Trails Club (BBTC).

THE HISTORY AND FUTURE OF RAIL-TRAILS

The first rail-trails were developed in the late 1960s and early 1970s. Creating these pioneering rail-trails was difficult because there were many questions about who would use them and what kinds of problems would develop. Yet most rail-trails have become dramatic successes, with high-volume usage and few management problems. The value of rail-trails has become more apparent in recent years. In 1987, the President's Commission on the American Outdoors recommended that "thousands of miles of abandoned railroads be converted to public use." Many articles have appeared about rail-trails in national magazines and local newspapers, and state and local agencies are learning that they are ideal public recreation facilities.

Washington has been a significant participant in this movement. Seattle's Burke–Gilman Trail, opened in 1976, was one of the first rail-trails in the United States. Today it serves more than 1 million users per year. The state has forty-eight rail-trails open to the public, covering more than 600 miles. They vary in length from half-mile-long sidewalks to a 130-mile route across the eastern part of the state.

There is a tremendous amount of support for rail-trails in Washington. The parks departments in Seattle, King County, and Bellingham have been building rail-trails for years. Surveys by counties also show that the most popular outdoor recreational activities are predominantly trail-use activities. A good indication of public support for continued development is passage of the 1989 King County open-space bond issue. This public bond issue passed by 82 percent and allocated $31 million for rail-trails and lowland trail development.

At the state level, several agencies manage rail-trails. The State Parks and Recreation Commission is pursuing development of its existing railroad rights-of-way for long-distance trails. The 1991 State Trails Plan also supports the creation of rail-trails. It calls for the State Parks and Recreation Commission to take the lead in creating rail-trails, adding another 450 miles of rail-trails and completing the Washington Cross-State Trail by the year 2000.

HOW YOU CAN HELP BUILD RAIL-TRAILS

There are several ways in which you can help build rail-trails. You can help organize or join a local citizen group that supports a specific rail-trail. Most rail-trail projects are local endeavors developed by cities or counties, and local support is critical to their success. The most successful rail-trails have had strong local coalitions formed solely to encourage their development. These include the following:

Cowiche Canyon Conservancy
Lower Yakima Pathway Coalition
Peninsula Trails Coalition
Pierce County Foothills Rails-to-Trails Coalition
Snohomish–Arlington Centennial Trail Coalition
Spokane River Centennial Trail Committee

You can talk to your elected city, county, and state officials and take them to where the proposed rail-trail will be constructed. Because these projects usually are government sponsored, it is vital to get the appropriate local agency and elected officials excited about rail-trails. The best way to do this is to take them for a walk on an existing rail-trail and show them the wonderful experience rail-trails provide.

You can encourage user groups to which you belong to support the development of rail-trails. Many user groups have an interest in trails. The following organizations support rail-trails in Washington State:

Backcountry Bicycle Trails Club (BBTC)
Backcountry Horsemen of Washington
Cascade Bicycle Club
Iron Horse Covered Wagon Association
John Wayne Pioneer Wagons and Riders
The Mountaineers
Transcontinental Trails Association
Pacific Regional Trails Council

You can volunteer to build rail-trails. The Volunteers for Outdoor Washington, The Mountaineers, Backcountry Horsemen of Washington, and the BBTC organize work parties to build rail-trails.

USING RAIL-TRAILS

A measure of the success of rail-trails is not just how many miles exist but how people use them. One benefit of a rail-trail is that its surface is wide enough to accommodate several users at once. For example, the Burke–Gilman Trail in Seattle is very popular and has both paved and gravel surfaces that accommodate walkers, runners, bicyclists, and skaters. Although the trail can be crowded at times, users have learned to follow the rules prescribed by the trail managers and to share the trail.

Trail Etiquette

One strength of rail-trails is that they can accommodate multiple uses. This increases support for their development by involving a wider range of citizens. But it is the responsibility of all users to learn and practice sharing the trails so that rail-trails are safe and enjoyable for all.

For these uses to coexist smoothly, it is important for users to follow proper trail rules and etiquette. No matter who uses these trails, common safety and courtesy rules help make the multiple-use concept work. These include general rules that all trail users should follow, as well as specific suggestions for the more popular trail uses.

General Rules

All trail users should observe the following rules:

∎ Obey posted trail rules.
∎ Pick up litter.
∎ Keep to the right of the trail.
∎ Let other trail users know when you are passing.
∎ Report trail damage to the trail manager.
∎ Respect the rights of property owners adjacent to the trail.
∎ Do not cross private property.
∎ Stay on the trail surface.
∎ Do not create your own path to waterways or sensitive areas next to the trail.
∎ Do not disturb wildlife or livestock.
∎ Close all gates that you pass through.
∎ Be courteous to other trail users.

Pedestrians and Hikers

Many people enjoy walking, and rail-trails are an ideal place for a long or short walk. Pedestrians, like other multiple-use trail users, must take responsibility to share the trail. Just because their mode of travel is more basic does not give them any more inherent right in the use of the trail over any other users.

▮ Do not cross through private property to get to the trail.

▮ Use the official trailheads or signed access points.

▮ Be aware of approaching bicycles and equestrians and do not make abrupt movements across the trail.

▮ On popular or crowded trails, leave room for other users to pass safely.

▮ Keep pets leashed and clean up after your animal.

Bicyclists

Rail-trails are ideal for bicycling because they do not have tight corners and have gentle grades. Bicyclists generally go faster than other trail users, so they must use special precautions.

▮ When overtaking another trail user, slow down, announce that you are passing by ringing a bell or by calling out "passing on your left," and then pass on the left.

▮ When approaching an oncoming bicyclist, move over to the right of the trail as far as is safe and ride single file.

▮ When approaching horses, slow down, then make human noises such as talking, singing, or whistling. If requested by the horseback rider, dismount and move your bicycle away from the horse on the downhill side of any hill.

▮ Be prepared by keeping your bicycle in good repair and carrying equipment to make small repairs.

Snohomish–Arlington Centennial Trail

▌ Always wear a helmet.
▌ Be kind to the earth; walk through very soft or muddy areas and don't skid your rear tire.

In-Line Skaters

In recent years in-line skating has become very popular. Paved rail-trails are one of the few safe and legal places for in-line skaters to travel long distances or go fast. Like other trail users, in-line skaters should proceed with care and use proper trail etiquette.

▌ When overtaking another trail user, slow down, announce which side you are passing on, and coast by, not taking a stride.
▌ Slow down in congested areas or in situations in which you may need to stop suddenly.
▌ Do not take strides when passing others in either direction.
▌ Wave faster cyclists around you; they will be unsure about passing when you are striding unless they know you are aware of them.

Equestrians

Equestrians find that rail-trails are one of the few public places they can take their horses for long rides. Where the trail surface is paved, many trail managers provide separate equestrian trails. Equestrians must be careful to observe trail rules to remain welcome on many of the rail-trails, both existing and under development.

▌ Obey trail signs for equestrians; use separate trailheads if available.
▌ Don't take shortcuts; stay on the trail or on a separate designated equestrian trail, if available.
▌ Walk your horse across bridges or steep grades.
▌ Keep your horse under control and at a walk around other trail users.
▌ Announce your intention to pass.
▌ Let other trail users know whether your horse is safe to pass.
▌ Stay out of soft, muddy areas.

Other Special Users

In addition to being popular with walkers, bicyclists, and equestrians, rail-trails are also extremely popular with special types of users, including the following:

▮ Families with strollers: Rail-trails are safe places for families with small children to take walks or ride bicycles.

▮ Wheelchair users: Racers and motorized wheelchair users find rail-trails one of few places they can travel safely yet be outside in a natural setting.

▮ Race-walkers: Rail-trails provide the gentle grade and even surface necessary for race-walking.

▮ Physically challenged: Because rail-trails are flat and often paved, people having difficulty walking because of age, disease, or injury find them a safe place to walk at their own speed.

▮ Horse-drawn-vehicle drivers: With the opening of the rail-trails in eastern Washington, horse-drawn wagons have been reborn in this state. Every year there is a wagon train ride across the state, and the drivers find rail-trails to be perfect for their needs. Drivers of horse-drawn sleighs also find them an ideal place to operate safely in the winter.

▮ Cross-country skiers: Rail-trails are gently sloped and generally safe from avalanches in the winter.

▮ Sled-dog mushers: These outdoor enthusiasts enjoy an easy route to run their dogs.

FUTURE RAIL-TRAILS

A number of rail-trails are planned for future development. Other rail-trail projects are in various stages of acquisition, planning, or development. These include the following:

Bay to Baker Rail-Trail
Black Diamond Trail
Lake Union Bikeway
Sedro-Woolley–Arlington Trail
Similkameen Trail
Whitehorse Trail
East Lake Sammamish Trail
Spokane–Newport Trail
Spokane–Cheney Trail
Enumclaw Trail
White River–Palmer Trail
Yelm–Tenino Trail
Klickitat Trail
Willapa Hills Trail

New rail-trails are being considered and constructed at an increasing pace as the demand for lowland trails increases. An attempt was made here to mention most of the rail-trail projects being developed in Washington today. If you know of other existing or planned rail-trails, please let the author know by contacting him through the Rail-Trail Resource Center on the World Wide Web at *www.rail-trail.org.*

PROPOSED RAIL-TRAILS

One purpose of this book is to show the location of rail-trails in Washington State and to entice people to use rail-trails. It is hoped that by using rail-trails, the public will understand their exceptional value and work to encourage the development of a complete statewide system of rail-trails for the enjoyment of Washington residents and visitors from other states and countries.

There are already more than 2000 miles of abandoned railroad rights-of-way in the state, with many more becoming available in the next few years. Together they create an opportunity to develop a complete system of interconnecting rail-trails throughout Washington.

The accompanying map illustrates the author's proposal for a statewide system of rail-trails. This proposal developed around ex-

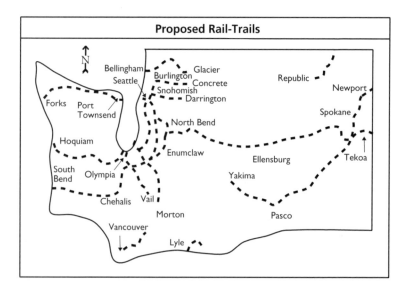

Proposed Rail-Trails

isting rail-trails, abandoned lines, and lines that probably will be abandoned. Many parts of this proposed system are already open to the public or plans are under way for developing a rail-trail. Together they can be developed into an interconnecting system of lowland trails throughout the state.

THE WASHINGTON CROSS-STATE TRAIL

Imagine walking, riding horseback, or bicycling all the way across Washington State on a nonmotorized path. This dream is becoming a reality with the development of the Washington Cross-State Trail, a series of rail-trails connecting the Pacific Ocean and Idaho. About 70 percent of the proposed route already is publicly owned. The most extensive portions open for public use are the Milwaukee Road Corridor Trail from Tekoa to the Columbia River and Iron Horse State Park from the Columbia River to Cedar Falls near North Bend. There are plans to add more miles westward in the next few years.

The interest in long-distance trails is becoming greater as more people look for places to enjoy the outdoors. There are now eight long-distance trail routes in the United States that are part of the National Scenic Trail System. Washington State has one National Scenic Trail, the Pacific Crest Scenic Trail, which runs along the

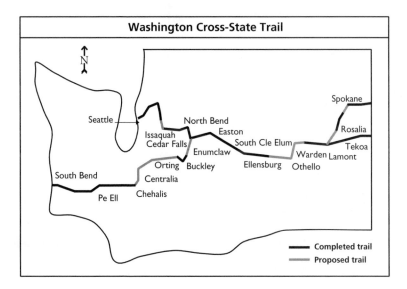

crest of the Cascade and Sierra Nevada ranges. There is also a pro-posal for a Pacific Northwest Trail that would cross the northern part of the state. One drawback is that both routes are under snow most of the year, and many portions of the trails are open only to foot and horse travel. The Washington Cross-State Trail would cre-ate a new world of long-distance trail possibilities, one that would be much more accessible to many people and open year-round.

The main route of the Washington Cross-State Trail passes through the towns of Tekoa, Rosalia, Warden, Othello, Ellensburg, South Cle Elum, Cedar Falls, Enumclaw, Buckley, Centralia, Chehalis, and South Bend. There will be a spur into Seattle and another through Spokane to Idaho. The following table outlines the existing individual trails that make up the Washington Cross-State Trail.

Iron Horse Trail near Ellensburg

Segment	From	To	Agency	Status
Washington Cross-State Trail				
Raymond–South Bend Trail	South Bend	Raymond	City of Raymond	Open
Willapa Hills Trail	Raymond	Chehalis	State Parks	Planned
Chehalis–Orting	Chehalis	Tenino	Thurston County	Missing link
Tenino–Yelm	Tenino	Yelm		Planned
Yelm to Orting	Yelm	Orting		Missing link
Foothills Trail	Orting	Buckley	Pierce County	Partially open
Buckley Trail	Buckley	White River	City of Buckley	Planned
Enumclaw Trail	White River	Enumclaw	City of Enumclaw	Planned
Enumclaw Plateau Trail	Enumclaw	Palmer	King County	Planned
Palmer to Cedar Falls	Palmer	Cedar Falls	King County	Missing link
Iron Horse State Park	Cedar Falls	Columbia River	State Parks	Open
Milwaukee Road Corridor Trail	Columbia River	Idaho	Dept. of Nat. Resources	Open seasonally
Seattle Spur				
Burke–Gilman Trail	Golden Gardens	Bothell	Seattle & King County	Partially open
Sammamish Slough Trail	Bothell	Redmond	King County	Open
East Lake Sammamish Trail	Redmond	Issaquah	King County	Planned
Issaquah Creek Trail	Issaquah	High Point	King County	Open
High Point–Preston	High Point	Preston	King County	Planned
Preston–Snoqualmie Trail	Preston	Snoqualmie	King County	Partially open
Snoqualmie Centennial Corridor Trail	Snoqualmie Falls	Snoqualmie	City of Snoqualmie	Open
Upper Snoqualmie Trail	Tokul Creek Road	Cedar Falls	King County	Partially open
Spokane Spur				
Spokane River Centennial Trail	Idaho	Spokane	State Parks	Open
Spokane Cheney Trail	Spokane	Cheney	Spokane County	Planned
Columbia Plateau Trail	Cheney	Cross-State Trail	State Parks	Partially open

The completion of the Washington Cross-State Trail will take the cooperation of many agencies. The Washington State Parks and Recreation Commission has taken a leadership role in this project. The 1991 State Trails Plan calls for completion of the Washington Cross-State Trail by the year 2000, with the Washington State Parks and Recreation Commission as the lead agency. The map on page 27 illustrates the proposed route of the Washington Cross-State Trail.

The Washington Cross-State Trail could connect through northern Idaho and Montana and help the development of the Trans-Continental Trail stretching from the Pacific to the Atlantic Ocean. The State of Idaho is working on building a trail from Plummer, near the end of the Washington Cross-State Trail, to Mullen, near the Montana border, a distance of 70 miles. Continuation of this route through Montana and North Dakota could link with the North Country Trail being developed between North Dakota and New York. The Trans-Continental Trail proposed by the author would be a valuable addition to our nation's National Scenic Trails System.

Milwaukee Corridor near Rosalia

how to use this book

At the beginning of this book is a map of Washington State showing the location of each rail-trail listed in the Contents. The text description of each rail-trail includes the following information:

■ **Trail name:** Each trail description includes the official trail name if an official name exists. For those with no formal name, a name that describes the trail location is used.

■ **Trail manager:** Included for each trail is the organization or agency responsible for managing the trail. The surface conditions, use restrictions, and degree of development of these trails are subject to change, so it is advisable to call or write the trail managers to get the most up-to-date information. A list of the names, addresses, and phone numbers of trail managers is provided in the Appendix.

■ **Endpoints:** The endpoints of a rail-trail are indicated, using city names or an easily identifiable geographic point. Sometimes the railroad grade goes beyond these official endpoints of the open portion of a trail route. It is also possible that these trails will be extended in the future, and the specified endpoints will change.

■ **Length:** The length of each rail-trail is indicated in miles for a one-way trip. The elevation gain or loss generally is not included because usually it is not significant.

■ **Surface:** There is wide variation in the surface condition of rail-trails, from paved 10- to 12-foot-wide asphalt paths to original railroad beds of rock ballast. The surface also can vary over the entire route of a particular trail. The predominant type of surface fits within one of four categories: asphalt or concrete, hard-packed gravel, unimproved ballast, or dirt. Although pedestrians can use all the surfaces, only the asphalt or concrete trails are suitable for road bikes (that is, bicycles with tires less than 1.5 inches wide). Even mountain bicyclists may find the loose gravel or unimproved ballast surfaces tough going. Equestrians may want to shy away from the asphalt or hard-packed gravel trails. Equestrians also should note that some ballast surfaces could be particularly hard on horses' hooves.

■ **Restrictions:** All the rail-trails listed in this book are closed to unauthorized motor vehicle use except the Republic Rail-Trail. Included for each trail are use restrictions made by the trail manager and recommendations about which modes of travel may be difficult.

■ **Original railroad:** The primary railroad company that built the original railroad is listed, as well as any other significant railroad history, such as the year of abandonment, if known.

■ **Location:** The nearest city and county are listed to help you identify the general trail location.

■ **Latitude/longitude:** Latitude and longitude in degrees are listed for use with global positioning systems (GPSs). The end of the trail first mentioned in the Endpoints section is given because it is usually the most desirable starting point.

■ **Elevation:** The elevation in feet of the lowest and highest points on the trial is indicated. With significant grade changes, both endpoint elevations are included. You cannot always calculate the actual slope from these two numbers because some rail-trails go up and down in elevation.

■ **Description:** There is much variation in the physical condition and ambience of these trails, from the concrete sidewalk of the Duwamish Bikeway to the wild, rugged natural terrain of the Milwaukee Road Corridor Trail. The description attempts to paint a verbal picture of each trail. Directions start from an interstate highway or a small community near the trail. These directions are to either the most popular trailhead or the one with the most parking. If appropriate, there is information on how to get to both ends of the trail and other good access points. Connections at both ends, intersections with other trails, and possible future links are noted.

■ **Map:** Included with each trail description is a map illustrating the entire route. This map shows roads, bodies of water, communities, and points of interest. For additional maps, call the trail manager listed at the top of each description (see the Appendix for addresses and phone numbers). Note that because many of these rail-trails are new, many do not appear on regular maps or show up as railroads.

Legend

Rail-trail	Mountain peak
Planned rail-trail	Cliff
Railroad	Mountain pass
Freeway	City/town
State highway	Park
Street/road	Former town
Water	Building
Trail	Location
	Private property

A NOTE ABOUT SAFETY

Safety is an important concern in all outdoor activities. No guidebook can alert you to every hazard or anticipate the limitations of every reader. Therefore, the descriptions of roads, trails, routes, and natural features in this book are not representations that a particular place or excursion will be safe for your party. When you follow any of the routes described in this book, you assume responsibility for your own safety. Under normal conditions, such excursions require the usual attention to traffic, road and trail conditions, weather, terrain, the capabilities of your party, and other factors. Keeping informed about current conditions and exercising common sense are the keys to a safe, enjoyable outing.

—*The Mountaineers Books*

part I

NORTHWEST WASHINGTON

1 Burlington Rail-Trail

Skagit County Parks and Recreation

Endpoint: Burlington
Length: 1.5 miles
Surface: gravel
Restrictions: none
Location: Burlington, Skagit County
Latitude/longitude: N48° 28.65'/W122° 19.32'
Elevation: 39 feet

This short community trail was built between a busy main state highway and an active Burlington Northern Santa Fe (BNSF) Railroad line. It provides a place for people to take a walk in an area of Burlington where there are no sidewalks along a main highway.

To get to the west end, from I-5 take exit 231 (marked Burlington). Go 1 mile east on SR 20 and turn right on North Regent Street. The local Lions Club has built a small park here, with picnic tables and

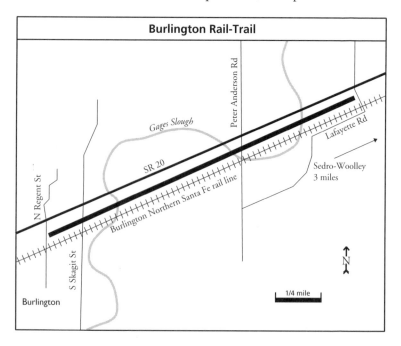

Taking a family stroll

shade trees. To get to the east end, continue on SR 20 for 1.5 miles and turn right on Lafayette Road. There is no parking area at this end.

The trail is crushed limestone that creates a hard surface that holds up well when it rains but is not suitable for skating or narrow-tire bicycles. There are plans for this trail to continue east through Sedro-Woolley and connect with the Cascade Trail.

2 Cascade Trail

Skagit County Parks and Recreation

Endpoints: Sedro-Woolley to Concrete
Length: 25 miles
Surface: gravel and paved
Restrictions: none
Location: Sedro-Woolley and Concrete, Skagit County
Latitude/longitude: N48° 30.80'/W122° 12.93'
Elevation: 68 feet at Sedro-Woolley, 228 feet at Concrete

Travel from farmland to the foothills of the Cascade Mountains on this long, scenic trail offering views of farms, the Skagit River, and the snow-capped Cascade Mountain peaks. This rail-trail provides a quiet pathway east from Sedro-Woolley, avoiding the busy and noisy SR 20. It gently transports you from farmland to the mountains.

To get to the west end, from I-5 take exit 231 (Burlington) and go east 5 miles to the eastern edge of Sedro-Woolley. As you leave the developed part of town, turn right on Polte Road. There is a gravel parking area just before this road where you can park between the trail and the highway. To get to the east end, continue east on SR 20 to Concrete. Turn left on 1st Street and immediately turn right into the parking lot of the Community Center building.

This railroad was built to carry lumber and farm goods to mills along the way. It also was used to haul concrete out from the town of Concrete. At one time the line was extended up to Nehalem during the construction of the dams above that town on the Skagit River.

Beginning outside Sedro-Woolley, the trail parallels the highway for a short way and then branches off through the woods and farmland. Most of the land adjacent to the trail is farmland, logged off a long time ago. But the railroad let the trees grow after the advent of diesel engines, and now there is a thick grove of deciduous trees along both sides of the right-of-way that is usually 100 feet wide. Often the tree cover is so thick that you cannot see out until you cross a clearing or creek. Cross a small bridge over an old oxbow of the river, and the trail skirts the Skagit River. Here is one of the best views to the east of the Cascade Mountains. There is a picnic bench, and it is a great place to relax and enjoy the river.

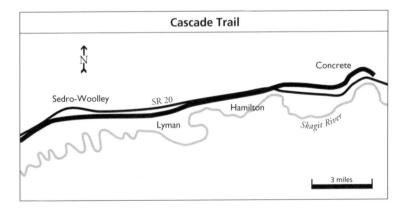

Walking the dog

Continuing east you will pass through the town of Lyman, one of the original station stops for the railroad. There is a grocery store on SR 20 due north. Pass more trees and farms, and the trail passes through the middle of Hamilton, a larger community that once had one of the largest logging mills on the line.

Soon after Hamilton the trail crosses SR 20 and parallels it to Concrete. The trail becomes almost imperceptibly steeper. Now the trail is lined with more evergreen trees and begins to traverse a hillside. After winding through the big trees, it comes out west of Concrete and you can see the rural sprawl of a formerly larger town. Continue past the main road crossing to First Street. Here you will find the old railroad depot, which has been restored and serves as a community center. There are bathrooms, picnic tables, and a nice grass lawn to rest on. If you are bicycling you will notice the grade on the return trip downhill to Sedro-Woolley.

There are plans to pave this trail, which would make it a great bike route for the cross-country travelers who now take SR 20 between Sedro-Woolley and Concrete. They will remember it fondly when climbing over Washington Pass on steep roads clogged with sightseers.

3 Dungeness River Bridge Trail

Jefferson County Parks Department

Endpoints: Dungeness River to East Runnion Road
Length: 0.5 mile
Surface: paved
Restrictions: none
Original railroad: North Coast Railway
Location: Sequim, Jefferson County
Latitude/longitude: N48° 5.14'/W123° 8.80'
Elevation: 203 feet

Although very short, this rail-trail is a great place to view the Dungeness River. The east end of the trail starts at the bridge over the Dungeness River. There is a long ramp that is accessible to wheelchair users. The large trees lining the riverbanks provide shade, and the water provides cooling on hot days. It is a wonderful place to take a short walk or to just stare at the river.

To get to the east end, from US 101 in Sequim, turn north on North 17th Avenue and left onto West Hendrickson Road for 1 mile. The trail begins at the end of the road. To get to the west end, from US 101 take Mill Road north about 0.5 mile and turn right on East Runnion Road. Go east about 0.25 mile until you see the end of the trail.

This trail is part of a proposed Olympic Discovery Trail that

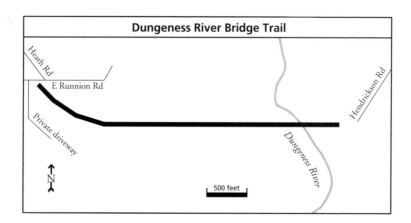

Dungeness River Bridge Trail

Heath Rd

E Runnion Rd

Private driveway

Hendrickson Rd

Dungeness River

N

500 feet

A group bicycle ride

may one day connect Port Townsend and Port Angeles. Other trails on this route are the Larry Scott Memorial Trail and the Port Angeles Urban Waterfront Trail.

4 Lake Whatcom Trail

Whatcom County Parks and Recreation

Endpoints: North Shore Road to Blue Canyon
Length: 3.0 miles
Surface: gravel
Restrictions: none
Original railroad: Lake Whatcom Railway
Location: Lake Whatcom, Whatcom County
Latitude/longitude: N48° 43.68'/W122° 18.22'
Elevation: 564 feet

This is a beautiful rail-trail alongside Lake Whatcom, far away from roads and houses. It skirts the lake beneath steep cliffs and is shaded by deciduous and evergreen trees. The rail-trail was built in 1991, with many slides cleared and creek crossings improved. A unique feature of the trail is that it can be accessed easily via water.

To get to the west trailhead, take Lake Whatcom North Shore Road to its end (including the new, wide road going uphill from the lake). The road crosses a creek and heads back down toward the lake, with the trailhead parking area on your left. There is no access from the east end.

The trail snakes beneath steep cliffs with occasional waterfalls

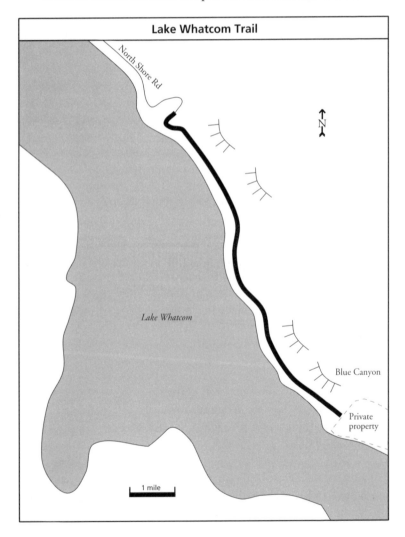

Lake Whatcom Trail

Looking west toward the trailhead

and several major stream crossings. There are no sandy beaches, although there are a few good water access points. The thick trees block most of the views across the lake but also provide excellent shade in the summer. The sight and sound of the water are a wonderful feature of this peaceful trail.

The rail-trail currently ends in 3 miles at private property. Please do not trespass. Whatcom County Parks and Recreation hopes to continue this trail east in the future.

5 Larry Scott Memorial Trail

Jefferson County Parks and Recreation

Endpoints: Port Townsend to Cape George Road
Length: 1.8 miles
Surface: gravel
Restrictions: none
Original railroad: North Coast Railway
Location: Port Townsend, Jefferson County
Latitude/longitude: N48° 6.15'/W122° 47.13'
Elevation: 32 feet at Port Townsend

This trail is part of the proposed Olympic Discovery Trail that could connect Port Townsend and Port Angeles. It is named after Larry

Scott, one of the founders of the Peninsula Trails Coalition, which first proposed this trail. It was named in memory of his efforts to get this trail built.

To get to the north end, take SR 20 into Port Townsend. At the bottom of the hill coming into town, turn right on Boat Street. Go one block and the trailhead is on the right at the end of Boat Street. To get to the south end, from SR 20 turn south on Mill Street, about 1 mile south of Boat Street.

This trail provides a great way to go for a walk or short bike ride away from downtown Port Townsend. It starts just south of the Port Townsend marina, which houses a wide variety of boats. Port Townsend is a popular place for working on wooden boats, and

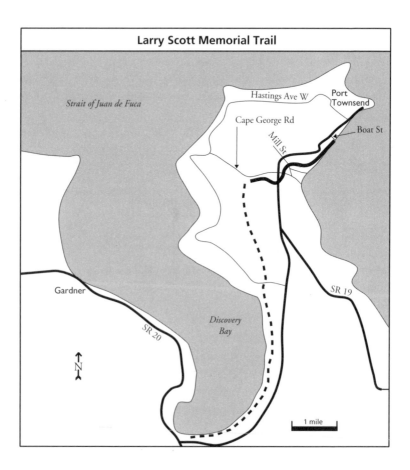

Larry Scott Memorial Trail

Strait of Juan de Fuca

Hastings Ave W

Port Townsend

Cape George Rd

Boat St

Mill St

Gardner

SR 19

SR 20

Discovery Bay

N

1 mile

Near Port Townsend, a family enjoys the view east.

there are many unusual examples near the trailhead. The trail begins right along the edge of the salt water and then begins to climb at the base of a steep, sandy slope. At the Port Townsend Paper Mill there is a viewpoint overlooking the bay with a good interpretive sign. This mill makes paper bags from recycled paper.

The trail then heads west, cutting along the side of a hill mostly sheltered by trees. It ends abruptly at Mill Road. If you continue south and west the railroad corridor is still in place, but it is unimproved as a trail. It is narrow and sandy and climbs at about 1 percent grade up to Cape George Road in another mile. Beyond this point it is partially blocked by an electric fence, so don't proceed. Jefferson County has control of the property down to Discovery Bay and plans to improve the trail to that point.

6 Old Robe Historic Trail

Snohomish County Parks and Recreation

Endpoints: Mountain Loop Highway to Tunnel #4
Length: 2.2 miles
Surface: dirt and rock, difficult footing in places
Restrictions: not recommended for bicycles or horses
Original railroad: Everett and Monte Cristo Railroad, built 1893, abandoned 1936
Location: 8.3 miles east of Granite Falls, Snohomish County
Latitude/longitude: N48° 6.60'/W121° 51.34'
Elevation: 1052 feet

Walk back in history to a rare place. This rail-trail follows the route of Everett and Monte Cristo Railroad, which was instrumental in the Monte Cristo gold rush. Monte Cristo was a booming mining community deep in the mountains east of Everett at the headwaters of the Stillaguamish River. The railroad was the critical link in getting the ore from the mines around Monte Cristo to the smelters in Everett. The line ran from Hartford (near the modern community of Lake Stevens) to Monte Cristo at the head of the valley. Hiking this rail-trail, you will be awed by the tenacity of the men who carved the railroad down the steep river canyon. It was very difficult to build and almost more difficult to keep open. Huge snowfalls caused avalanches, and flooding tore out land underneath the rail bed and created landslides.

The rail-trail has a gentle grade, but the surface is as tough as the country it passes through. Be prepared for rough footing and, in places, steep drop-offs to the river. The land is so steep that many tunnels were built along this route. Three of those tunnels are part of the experience on this rail-trail. You also can see how a roadbed was carved out of the bedrock alongside the river, with the troughs cut for ties still evident.

To get to the trailhead, take Mountain Loop Highway 8.3 miles east of Granite Falls to the top of the long, steep hill. On the south side of the road (across from Forest Service Road 41) is a sign inscribed on a section of log marking the start of the Old Robe Historic Trail.

The trail starts out through a clear-cut with high bushes, moves through deep trees, and joins the railroad grade in 0.2 mile. It moves out into a wide, flat bog area, the site of the original community of Robe. It remains smooth, wide, and flat until it joins the river at 0.7 mile. Then steep hillsides and the results of years of erosion take over. There are several areas that are always wet, several stream crossings, and many rocky areas that demand good balance and sure-footedness. If it has been raining recently, you also may have to walk through a small waterfall. This trail has not been improved except by the users.

At mile 1.2 you can see where the rock was chiseled out to hold the railway ties. The rock is preserved in the exact shape of the old

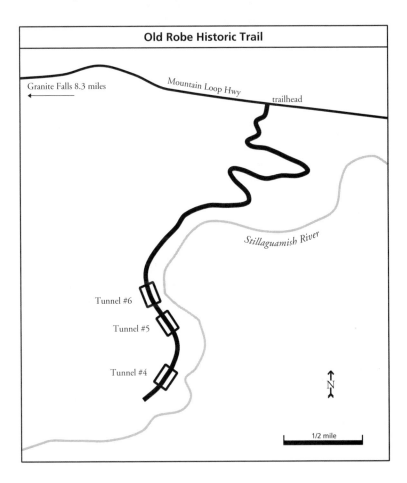

Snow along the Stillaguamish River

ties just inches from the river gorge. Here the river gets very narrow and noisy, and the old railroad had to go through the hills to fit in the canyon. The first tunnel is called tunnel #6, the sixth tunnel from Hartford (now Lake Stevens) and the start of the line. Tunnel #6 is about 250 feet long, on a slight curve, and with enough light even in the deep forest for claustrophobic visitors not to get nervous. At mile 1.7 is tunnel #5, 100 feet long and straight. Imagine carving these tunnels with hand tools! The next tunnel, #4, was removed by the railroad and is now a cut with a rockslide at the west end.

Just beyond this point is a huge rock wall built up from the river to the grade. It supported a wooden structure holding up the rails and prevented erosion by the river. Farther along is tunnel #3, which has collapsed.

Caution: The trail becomes dangerous beyond this point, and only visitors experienced in off-trail scrambling should proceed.

One of the pleasures of this rail-trail is traveling next to the Stillaguamish River as it carves through the narrow canyon. It is very noisy as it plunges down through the canyon, and you can hear the echo off the rock walls next to the trail. It is also easy to understand why the railroad was abandoned after many accidents caused by floods, avalanches, and slides.

The Old Robe Preservation Society is working on expanding this trail from the west. Going east from this trailhead, the existing highway follows the old railroad grade almost all the way to Barlow Pass. From Barlow Pass you can walk or bike up to the old Monte Cristo town site, which is open to the public for viewing in the summer. It is operated by the Monte Cristo Preservation Society and has a fascinating exhibit of old mining equipment and historical displays.

7 Port Angeles Urban Waterfront Trail

City of Port Angeles Parks and Recreation

Endpoints: ITT Rayonier Mill site to Coast Guard Station
Length: 5.8 miles
Surface: asphalt
Restrictions: none
Location: Port Angeles, Clallam County
Latitude/longitude: N48° 7.20'/W123° 25.80'
Elevation: 28 feet

This is a true waterfront trail with views everywhere. The rail-trail starts out at the vertex of waterfront congestion near the ferry terminal to Victoria and the city pier on Railroad Avenue. There are shops, motels, and restaurants, as well as a viewing platform and a sandy beach. After a few moments of walking on the trail, you are away from all the noise and congestion and can continue peacefully along the water's edge. This is an ideal place for a stroll, with views across the Strait of Juan de Fuca. It is also a popular place for short bike rides.

To find this rail-trail, go to Port Angeles and turn north on Lincoln Street to the waterfront (follow the signs for the Victoria ferry). The logical starting point is at Lincoln Street and Railroad Avenue. There is also access at the north end of Francis Street.

There are two different directions to go from this starting point, with completely different atmospheres. If you head east the trail is right on the water for 1.5 miles. The rail-trail follows closely along the water's edge, barely 5 feet above the water at high tide. You are so close you can smell the salt air, hear the ferry whistles, and view the distant mountains of Vancouver Island. On a clear day you can see the city of Victoria across the Strait of Juan de Fuca. The trail is shaded by the steep hillside on the south and can be cold and damp most days. Currently the trail ends at the old ITT Rayonier Mill site, but there are plans to continue this trail another 3 miles along the water east up Morse Creek to US 101.

If you head west, the trail is a wide, paved sidewalk on the north side of Railroad Avenue. Follow the signs and pathway as it winds around onto Marine Drive past old industrial areas and a marina. In about a mile the trail turns north out onto Ediz Hook. Pass by a grassy area with a viewpoint of the bay, and then the trail crosses over to the north side of Marine Drive and enters the Dai-showa Mill. Be very careful passing through the mill site and watch carefully for the trail markings on the asphalt. This is a working mill with lots of noisy machinery. Stay between the yellow lines and watch carefully for trucks crossing.

Beyond the mill the trail runs adjacent to Marine Drive on the south side. There is a boat launch and park, and just before the Coast Guard Station is a picnic area. The views from here are spectacular: looking southwest at the Olympic Mountains, north to Vancouver

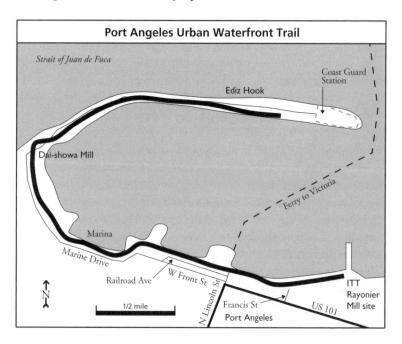

A chilly morning stroll along the waterfront

Island, or east to Mount Baker. This is a great place to relax and enjoy being near the water with all its wildlife and boat traffic.

This rail-trail is very popular with local citizens on lunch breaks and with the numerous tourists who are waiting for the ferry or exploring Port Angeles. The trail is part of the Olympic Discovery Trail that someday may connect Port Angeles with Port Townsend.

8 Railroad Bikeway

City of Bellingham Parks and Recreation

Endpoints: Memorial Park to Lake Whatcom
Length: 4.0 miles
Surface: gravel and dirt
Restrictions: dogs on leash only, no horses
Original railroad: Bellingham Bay & Eastern Railway
Location: Bellingham, Whatcom County
Latitude/longitude: N48° 45.98'/W122° 27.79'
Elevation: 147 feet at King Street, 320 feet at Lake Whatcom

This is a quiet neighborhood trail from central Bellingham to Lake Whatcom. It has a fine view west of Bellingham to the San Juan

Islands and connects Memorial Park with Lake Whatcom Park. There is good wildlife viewing in the deep forest area near Lake Whatcom, which includes several other trails, a dam, and a waterfall.

The people who live in the neighborhood use this trail a great deal for long walks. It is also a popular bike route, offering a safe, gentle, scenic east–west route across I-5 and Bellingham. Although the surface is not paved, it is usually suitable for skinny-tired bikes. The trail passes an elementary school and provides a safe route for children, off busy streets.

To get to the west trailhead, take I-5 to exit 255 (Sunset Drive). Turn left (west) on Sunset Drive to James Street. Turn left (south) on James Street and left (east) on Maryland. Go one block to King Street and Memorial Park. The trailhead is on King Street between North Street and Connecticut. To get to the east trailhead, park in the west

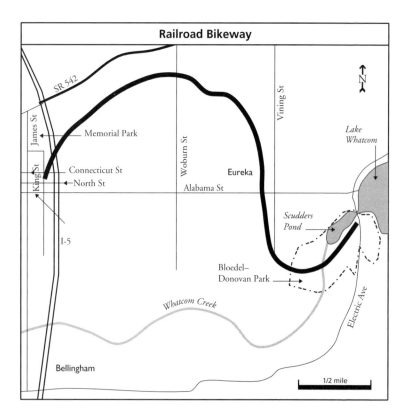

Railroad Bikeway

A sunny fall hike along Scudders Pond

side parking area at the intersection of Electric Avenue and Alabama Street at the west end of Lake Whatcom.

The trail starts at Memorial Park near I-5, crosses over an old railway span, and heads into a residential street. Because the railroad right-of-way is 100 feet wide, there is a buffer of shrubs and trees from most homes and the grade school. The trail crosses a broad meadow and a small flood control dam, with an opportunity for bird watching. Farther along, the route provides excellent views looking west over Bellingham to the San Juan Islands.

There is a dangerous crossing at Alabama Street that is a steep main arterial with fast traffic. There is no trail crossing marked between the sidewalks, so be very careful crossing Alabama Street. Once across, enter a narrow, winding portion through the woods before breaking out next to a new housing development. This is your last lookout to the west, with views of the San Juan Islands. The trail then enters the deep woods of Bloedel–Donovan Park. This is a wonderful wooded area with a deep ravine and Whatcom Creek. There is a Y-junction in the trail, with the south spur leading to an old railroad trestle. Stay left (north) and come to Scudder's Pond. This small pond is named after the person who gave it to the city and is maintained by the North Cascades Audubon Society. It is home to many birds, and the local Audubon group has improved the trail alongside it. The rail-trail ends at Electric Avenue and Alabama Street. Just across the street, on the shores of Lake Whatcom, is a more developed portion of the park, with restrooms, picnic tables, and an old steam engine that used to ply this line.

9 South Bay Trail

City of Bellingham Parks and Recreation

Endpoints: Fairhaven to Bellingham
Length: 1.7 miles
Surface: loose gravel
Restrictions: no horses
Original railroad: Bellingham Bay & Eastern Railway
Location: Bellingham, Whatcom County
Latitude/longitude: N48° 43.24'/W122° 30.25'
Elevation: 58 feet at Fairhaven, 41 feet at Bellingham

This delightful trail connects Fairhaven with downtown Bellingham via the waterfront. The trail has great views and passes through Boulevard Park and near the Waterfront Park viewpoint. It is a popular trail for walking because of its outstanding views and the amenities of Fairhaven, Bellingham, and Boulevard Park. Mountain bicyclists will enjoy it as an interesting way to travel between Bellingham and Fairhaven. It is not suitable for road bikes or horses.

To get to the southern trailhead, take I-5 to Bellingham and exit 250 (Old Fairhaven Parkway) into the Fairhaven District. Turn right onto South State Street and left on Mill Avenue. The trail starts at the intersection of 10th Street and Mill Avenue, although you can park anywhere in the Fairhaven District. Fairhaven is a small community just south of downtown Bellingham that has been designated as a National Historic District. It has old, renovated buildings full of restaurants and shops. It is a fascinating place to visit at the start or finish of your trail trip.

The gravel trail heads north and winds along the top of the cliff. In the future it will turn west onto the public dock and go along the waterfront. In the interim it returns briefly to a quiet side street and then heads steeply downhill and crosses the main-line Burlington

Northern tracks. Use caution when crossing these tracks. There are plans to use an existing overpass just south of here to cross the tracks.

Part of the rail-trail is built over the water on the original pilings used by the railroad. This is a wonderful spot, especially for

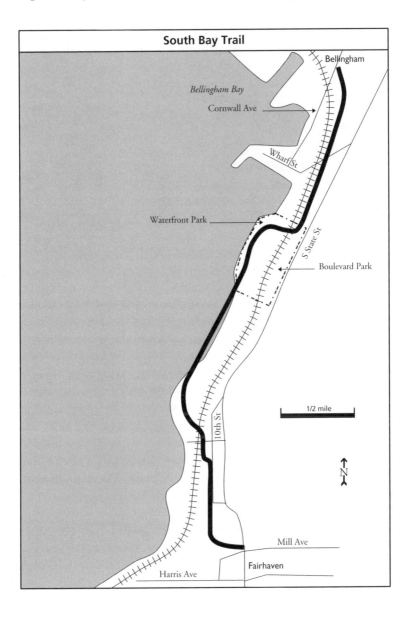

Bicycling the bridge over the bay

fishers, who sometimes crowd the walkway. The trail enters Boulevard Park, a large developed area with all the usual park amenities.

Heading north out of Boulevard Park, cross over the active Burlington Northern tracks. *Caution:* This is the main-line track again, so look carefully both directions and cross carefully. There is a beautiful wooden overpass designed for pedestrian use, but it doesn't connect directly with the rail-trail. The route follows the steep bank above the water and comes into the south end of downtown Bellingham. A side route uphill connects with Waterfront Park, an overlook of Bellingham Bay. This area has a small shelter with a tremendous view of Bellingham Bay and the San Juan Islands. Continue north, crossing Wharf Street, and the trail takes you directly into downtown Bellingham at Cornwall Avenue.

To the south the trail connects with the Whatcom County Interurban Trail via the Lower Padden Creek Trail. From Fairhaven, continue south on 10th Street and look for the signs for Lower Padden Creek Trail.

10 Spruce Railroad Trail

Olympic National Park

Endpoints: East Beach Road to Camp David Jr Road
Length: 4.0 miles
Surface: dirt, rugged in places
Restrictions: no firearms, no pets, horses not advised
Original railroad: Spruce Railroad, built 1918, abandoned 1954, trail opened 1982
Location: Lake Crescent, Clallam County
Latitude/longitude: N48° 5.43'/W123° 48.09'
Elevation: 712 feet

This is a delightful trail along the shores of beautiful Lake Crescent, so named because of its shape. It provides a great view and access to Lake Crescent, as well as a peaceful place to stroll. The trail is heavily used by hikers visiting Olympic National Park and is also ideal for mountain bikes. The trail was constructed in 1982 by the National Park Service.

The original railroad was constructed in 1918 in only five months by the U.S. Army from Port Angeles to 36 miles west. The reason for the hurry was that the Olympic Peninsula had one of the few good stands of spruce wood, used to build airplanes. World War I ended a few weeks before the railroad was completed, but the railroad hauled logs for the next thirty years.

There is good access at both ends of this trail. To get to the east end, go west on Highway 101 from Port Angeles and turn north just before Lake Crescent onto East Beach Road. At 3.3 miles, turn left and follow the signs to the Spruce Railroad Trail. To get to the west end, drive on Highway 101 past Lake Crescent and turn north on Camp David Jr Road, the first road past the end of the lake. Stay left at the Y and go 4.9 miles to the end of the road and the trailhead.

The vegetation along the trail is not typical of the Olympic Peninsula. Because of the low elevation (580 feet) and the rain shadow effect, parts of the trail are open forest with a different microclimate. There are species uncommon to the Olympics, including poison oak and madrone trees. This area is notorious for ticks, so take precautions.

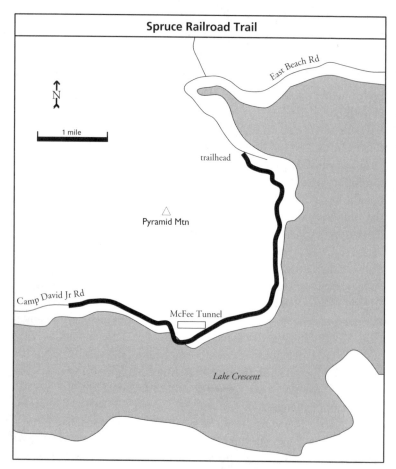

Spruce Railroad Trail

1 mile

trailhead

△
Pyramid Mtn

Camp David Jr Rd

McFee Tunnel

Lake Crescent

The west end of the trail starts at the east end of a National Park Service parking area and goes up a short gravel path to the warning signs about poison oak and ticks. At both trailheads you'll find an informative brochure made available by the Pacific Northwest National Parks and Forests Association describing the history of the railroad, with some excellent photographs.

At mile 1.0 the trail bypasses the 460-foot McFee Tunnel and drops down to the lake. There the National Park Service has built a steel-and-wood bridge across a short cliff area. The lake is so clear

Bridge bypassing tunnel

that you can see more than 40 feet down into the light-blue waters. The lake is known for this clear water and its depth. Across the lake to the south you can hear the rumbling of logging trucks and see the Lake Crescent Lodge. There is also an occasional motorboat.

The trail follows the old railway grade except where it passed through two tunnels. Generally the grade is wide, hard-packed dirt, showing the volume of use the trail receives. Be careful while circumventing the tunnels because the trail becomes more difficult, steep, and narrow.

Although the trail stops at the west end where Camp David Jr Road ends, the railroad grade does not. Abandoned in 1954, the grade itself is in excellent shape and ready for continued use. There are plans to continue this trail west to Forks and east to Port Angeles and the Port Angeles Waterfront Trail.

11 Whatcom County Interurban Trail

Whatcom County Parks and Recreation

Endpoints: Fairhaven to Larrabee State Park
Length: 5.5 miles
Surface: hard-packed gravel and dirt
Restrictions: none
Original railway: Interurban Railway
Location: Fairhaven, Whatcom County
Latitude/longitude: N48° 42.94'/W122° 29.72'
Elevation: 108 feet at Old Fairhaven Parkway, 162 feet at Chuckanut Drive

The Whatcom County Interurban Trail is a wonderful alternative to the ups and downs of Chuckanut Drive, providing a gentle, shaded grade. The rail-trail clings to the steep hillside above Chuckanut Drive, and the fact that the railroad grade is still there, whereas Chuckanut Drive continues to fall into the sea, is evidence of the good engineering and construction of the railroad. This rail-trail provides access to deep woods, creeks, and views of the San Juan Islands and connects to Larrabee State Park and the beach.

The north trailhead is reached from I-5 by taking exit 250

(Chuckanut Drive, Old Fairhaven Parkway) and going 0.7 mile west on Old Fairhaven Parkway. Look for a large trail sign on the south side of the road and park along the road. To reach the south trailhead, take Chuckanut Drive (SR 11) to Larrabee State Park. Use the main entrance and park at the first parking lot. The trailhead and sign are directly across the road from the park entrance.

Starting from the north, the trail passes through the backyards of local homes, hidden by the thick trees on both sides. It climbs gently into deep woods and descends to Padden Creek, where there used to be a large trestle, long removed. Then climb out of the creek

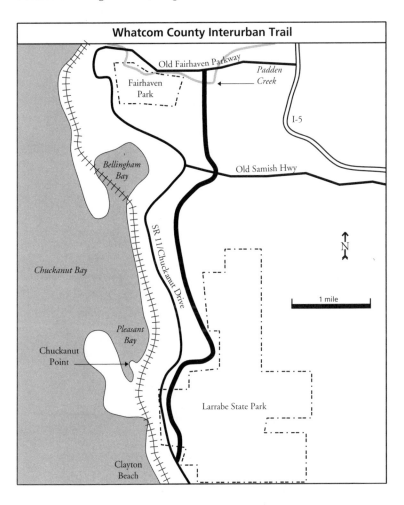

bed and find a smooth, flat dirt path to the crossing of Old Samish Highway. South of this crossing the woods thin out and you begin to get glimpses of Bellingham Bay and the San Juan Islands in the distance. The canopy of trees makes it a wonderful place to be in the heat of the summer, and because most of the trees are deciduous, it is a wonderfully scenic place to be in fall. In the winter, the views to the west open up after the leaves have fallen.

Cyclists heading south from Old Fairhaven Parkway

Continuing south the trail is on a steep side slope. The trail's gentle grade in such steep terrain is appreciated by nonmotorized users of the trail. The trail follows the contour of the land and heads west above Chuckanut Point. Here there are views west to Wildcat Cove far below. The Fragrance Lake Trail crosses and heads uphill to Fragrance Lake. This is a hiker-only trail that also goes downhill to the Larrabee State Park parking area. In 0.25 mile is the end of the trail at Chuckanut Drive.

This trail gets heavy use from Bellingham residents. It has many access points, so pedestrians can use it easily. It is very popular with runners, and several 10-kilometer races are held on it every year. Mountain bicyclists find the trail ideal because it leads to numerous trails in the hills above Larrabee State Park.

At the south end, you can cross Chuckanut Drive to a trail leading down to Clayton Beach at Larrabee State Park. The Clayton Beach Trail is the southward extension of the Interurban Railroad right-of-way. This is the same interurban line that ran all the way to Tacoma, and the Interurban Trail of Snohomish County and the King County Interurban Trail also use portions of the same line.

The Whatcom County Interurban Trail is a result of the cooperative efforts of Whatcom County Parks, Washington State Parks and Recreation Commission, and Puget Power and Light and is a wonderful addition to the Bellingham area trail system.

part II
PUGET SOUND

12 Burke—Gilman Trail

City of Seattle SeaTrans Department, King County Parks

Endpoints: Eighth Avenue Northwest in Ballard to Bothell
Length: 17.0 miles
Surface: 8- to 12-foot-wide asphalt; gravel path alongside part way
Restrictions: no horses, 15-mph speed limit, dogs on leash
Original railroad: Seattle, Lake Shore & Eastern Railroad, abandoned 1971; trail opened 1976
Location: Seattle, King County
Latitude/longitude: N47° 39.68'/W122° 22.23'
Elevation: 28 feet at 11th Avenue Northwest, 58 feet at Bothell

The Burke–Gilman Trail is one of the oldest and most popular rail-trails in the United States and a wonderful example of an urban rail-trail. It is a preferred bicycle commuting route also used by walkers, recreational bicyclists, roller-skaters, runners, race-walkers, wheelchair users, and even mothers on skates pushing large-wheeled baby carriages. More than 1 million users per year enjoy this popular trail, as counted every five years by the Cascade Bicycle Club. Almost everyone who has lived in the area for a while knows about the "BG," as it is called.

The name of the trail comes from the founders of the railroad, Judge Thomas Burke and Daniel Gilman. They started the Seattle, Lake Shore & Eastern Railroad in 1885 to haul goods and passengers around Lake Washington. This railroad is mentioned often in this book because it was responsible for many of the old routes around Seattle that have now become rail-trails.

The trail is most popular with bicyclists, who make up more than 80 percent of all trail users on the Burke–Gilman Trail. It makes a wonderful bypass of the hilly and busy Lake City Way and is an excellent way to get around the north end of Lake Washington because bicycles are excluded from the Evergreen Point Floating Bridge. It is also popular going west from the university because most streets go up and down over steep hills.

The numerous access points and dense population along the entire route are one reason the Burke–Gilman Trail is so popular, although half the users drive to get to the trail. The trail has become so popular with nearby neighbors that many have constructed small, informal access trails from their property to the trail to make it easier for them to enjoy.

Five major parks border the route: Gasworks Park, Magnuson Park, Matthews Beach Park, Tracey Owen Station, and Blyth Park. These make great destinations or picnic stops, but the rail-trail itself is also a park that traverses steep ravines and creeks and often passes under canopies of trees. It is a cool place on hot days and provides shelter from the wind on stormy days.

Although the trail extends west to Eighth Avenue Northwest,

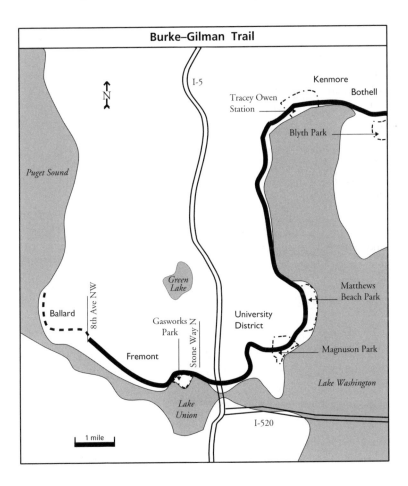

the most popular trailhead for going east and north is at Gasworks
Park at the north end of Lake Union in Wallingford. Take I-5 to exit
169 (45th Street); turn west and proceed about 1 mile to Stone Way
North and then turn south (left) onto Stone Way North. Proceed to
the bottom of the hill and turn left on Boat Street (across Pacific
Street), continuing east four blocks to Gasworks Park. The trail is
actually across the north side of Boat Street and does not enter Gasworks Park. To get to the east end of the Burke–Gilman Trail in
Bothell, from I-5 take Lake City Way (exit 171, SR 522) to Bothell
and turn right on Northeast 180th Street in Bothell. Park at the Bothell
Landing Park just south of the bridge. The Burke–Gilman Trail begins just south of this parking area to the west of Northeast 180th
Street. The Sammamish Slough Trail begins here and continues east
to Redmond.

Gasworks Park is the site of an old power-generating facility
that developed electricity by burning coal taken from the Newcastle
mines and barged across Lake Washington from the present-day
Newport area of Bellevue. Gasworks Park has a spectacular view of
Seattle and Lake Union, with its crowded boat traffic, water access,
and great kite flying. You can watch power boats, sailboat races
(called the Duck Dodge because of the crowded conditions) on Tues-
days in the summer, floatplanes departing for points north, and kites
on windy days.

About 1 mile east of Gasworks Park the trail passes through
the University District, crossing "The Ave" (University Way). This
area has shops, restaurants, and the changing flavor of a university. Between the University Way and 15th Avenue crossings is a
small park, adjacent to the trail, named the Bob Pyle Wilderness
after a University of Washington student who became famous as a
butterfly expert.

The trail is heavily used by university students and staff for commuting, walking through campus, and exercising. The trail passes
the Hec Edmundson Pavilion and Husky Stadium, where a footbridge spans busy Montlake Boulevard Northeast. This footbridge
is the safest bicycle route for those going south over Montlake Bridge;
just stay on the east side of Montlake Boulevard Northeast. There
are mileage markers beginning at Gasworks Park and a variety of
mileage markers beginning at the overpass near the Hec Edmundson

Pavilion on the University of Washington campus.

Where the trail crosses 40th Avenue Northeast is the small Burke–Gilman Park, with a playground, picnic benches, and a creek alongside it. Beyond this point the trail enters deep woods and divides for a short distance into two one-way lanes. There is also a gravel path on one and sometimes both sides of the paved surface that is especially popular with runners.

Magnuson Park is a large natural area and park on Lake Washington with a swimming beach, boat launch, tennis courts, and restrooms. The park can be accessed by leaving the trail at the Northeast 65th Street crossing and going downhill across Sand Point Way Northeast.

At mile 7.1 the trail skirts Matthews Beach Park. This is the last public access to Lake Washington for several miles. This park has restrooms, playgrounds, picnic tables, and a shallow, sandy beach.

Commuters riding by the University of Washington

Next the trail passes through a residential area with narrow private-access driveways. You can get glimpses of Lake Washington between and over the tops of houses. At mile 10.0 the trail leaves the Seattle city limits and is under the jurisdiction of King County.

At mile 11.9 is a side trail to Tracey Owen Station, a small park next to the water. There are restrooms, picnic tables, bike racks, water access via a sandy beach, ducks, and a view of Lake Washington. Beyond this park the trail crosses under Juanita Drive through a long, bright tunnel. It then parallels busy Northeast Bothell Way (SR 522) before dropping below the road grade.

At mile 14.5 there is a tunnel under 96th Avenue Northeast. Continue straight and just outside the tunnel cross the Sammamish Slough on an old railroad bridge. Just before the bridge is a side trail to the north that takes you to Bothell Landing, a City of Bothell park on the Sammamish Slough. Just after the railway trestle is Blyth Park on your right. Keep on the trail at Northeast 180th Street, turn north (left), and connect with the Sammamish Slough Trail by turning left into a parking lot. This trail continues 12 miles into Redmond. If completed, the planned East Lake Sammamish Trail would continue this rail-trail route to Issaquah.

From Gasworks Park you can also travel west. This part of the trail is under development, with many changes, and it may not be exactly as described here. Going west from Gasworks Park the trail is on the north side of Boat Street and then passes behind some buildings before crossing Stone Way North. The trail hugs the retaining wall on the south side of North 34th Street and then abruptly turns to the water and hugs the water's edge. This is not the original railroad alignment; a large developer removed all the buildings in this industrial area and has put up new office buildings, obliterating the old grade. However, the old line went through a tunnel under the Fremont Bridge (as it still does on the south side of the ship canal) and between steep walls and buildings. The current route is much more scenic. It continues west along the ship canal with picnic benches, grass, and places to watch the boats going by.

At 3rd Avenue Northwest the rail line pulls away from the water and passes through an industrial area with a variety of businesses on both sides. It currently ends at 8th Avenue Northwest but it maybe extended to 11th Avenue Northwest by the time you read this book. The City of Seattle has plans to complete this trail along the railroad right-of-way all the way to Golden Gardens Park on Puget Sound.

Because of the high volume of use and variety of users, there is the potential for overcrowding and conflicts between users. The trail managers have posted signs and trail rules that have helped reduce problems. Trail users generally follow the rules, with bicyclists and in-line skaters calling out "On your left" or ringing a bell when passing. The City of Seattle Police and Animal Control officers patrol the trail on mountain bikes. Please do your part to share this great trail responsibly.

13 Cedar River Trail

King County Parks and Recreation

Endpoints: Renton to Landsburg
Length: 16.0 miles
Surface: paved and gravel
Restrictions: none
Original railroad: Chicago, Milwaukee and St. Paul Railroad
Location: Renton and Maple Valley, King County
Latitude/longitude: N47° 28.82'/W122° 12.00'
Elevation: 72 feet at Renton, 537 feet at Landsburg

This trail transports you from the noisy freeways of Renton up the Cedar River to the foothills of the Cascades. It is a combination urban and rural route that includes a paved section from Renton to Maple Valley and then gravel to the end of the trail at Landsburg.

To get to the west trailhead in Renton, from I-405 in Renton, turn east on SR 169. Take the first right into the Cedar River Park to the south of Highway 169. This park has a recreation center, restrooms, picnic tables, soccer fields, and phones. Keep to the right of the main building and follow the roadway around behind the building; park behind the building. The trail begins under I-405 on a bridge across the Cedar River. To get to the east trailhead, take SR 169 east to SR 516 and turn east to Georgetown. Turn left at Georgetown on 276th Avenue Southeast and head north. The road turns into Landsburg Road and crosses the Cedar River. There is parking on the west side of Landsburg Road on the north side of the Cedar River.

If you begin in Renton, you will cross a bridge built on the old I-405 bridge abutments. Turn east upriver and enjoy the immediate escape from the noise of the freeway as you follow the trail high above the river. About 1 mile upriver is Riverview Park, with picnic tables, restroom, a phone, and parking off of SR 169. The trail then crosses the Cedar River on an old railroad bridge that is a great place to watch salmon during the fall. The trail curls around and under SR 169 and parallels a golf course. At Ron Regis Park there are restrooms and ballfields. The pavement ends at Cedar Grove Road Southeast.

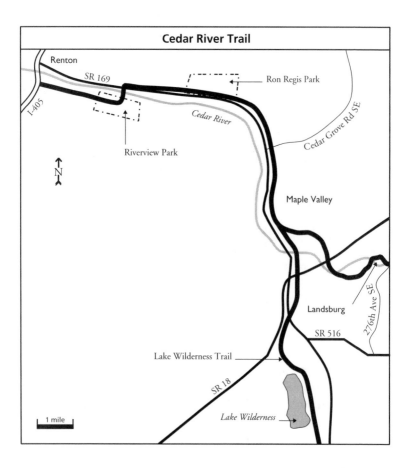

Cedar River Trail

The Cedar River near Landsburg

The trail continues east parallel to busy SR 169, climbing gradually to Maple Valley. At Maple Valley, once you have crossed the bridge over the Cedar River, you can get onto the Lake Wilderness Trail by keeping to the right. Continuing east, the trail is gravel and passes through a forest with occasional glimpses of the river. It winds back and forth across the Cedar River three times on its way to Landsburg.

The trail stops at Landsburg because the City of Seattle Water Department does not want the public in the watershed used for the region's water system. In a few years the water will be filtered, so this trail may be extended through the watershed to Cedar Falls to connect with Iron Horse State Park at Rattlesnake Lake. A portion of this segment would become part of the Washington Cross-State Trail.

14 Coal Creek Trail

King County Parks

Endpoints: Newcastle Coal Creek Road to Coal Creek Parkway
Length: 3.0 miles
Surface: dirt and gravel
Restrictions: no bicycles
Original railroad: Seattle and Walla Walla Railroad, built 1878
Location: south side of Cougar Mountain, King County
Latitude/longitude: N47° 32.08'/N47° 32.08'
Elevation: 669 feet

The history of the coal era in Puget Sound lies buried along this trail, with some relics of the past still visible. The Newcastle town site was the terminus of the Seattle and Walla Walla Railroad, which hauled coal from the Newcastle mines to the wharfs of Seattle. It is a quiet place for a walk in a historic location. The trail is located in the upper reaches of Coal Creek, aptly named after the rich coal-producing area from which it flows.

To find the east trailhead, take the Newport Way Southeast exit from I-405 and proceed east to Newcastle Coal Creek Road. Turn left (north) on Newcastle Coal Creek Road to where it crosses Coal Creek (a tight corner). Park in the parking area for Cougar Mountain County Park and cross Newcastle Coal Creek Road. Go across a small meadow and look for a sign marked Coal Creek Trail. To get to the west end, from I-405 take the Newport Way Southeast exit and proceed east, keeping right at Coal Creek Parkway. When the road drops suddenly across Coal Creek there is a small gravel parking area on the east side. The trail heads up the creek on the north side.

The best place to start is from the east end, where there are good interpretive signs. On the south side of the creek is the site of the coal dumps, where coal was loaded from mine cars onto main-line railroad cars. There is also evidence of the shoring used to build over the creek, and there are still some artifacts in the bushes. One mine entrance is still partially visible, but the vegetation that has finally had an opportunity to grow has covered up almost all human impact on this narrow creek bed.

The trail heads west across a broad meadow and then back into the deep woods. It is rough in places, but is possible to proceed west to Coal Creek Parkway, where there is a small gravel parking area.

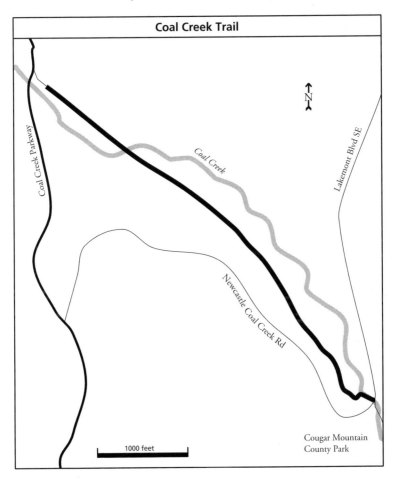

Coal Creek Trail

The trail is located in a King County park, although it has not been well developed. An interpretive center for relics collected by the Newcastle Historical Society would be a useful addition. This railroad grade continues down to Lake Washington, and perhaps more of it will be developed for public use in the future.

Hiking in the darkness of the Coal Creek overgrowth

15 Duwamish Bikeway

City of Seattle Engineering Department

Endpoints: 65th Avenue Southwest to Michigan Street
Length: 6.8 miles
Surface: asphalt and concrete
Restrictions: none
Original railroad: Seattle & San Francisco Railway & Navigation Co., built 1903
Location: Seattle, King County
Latitude/longitude: N47° 34.66'/W122° 24.92'
Elevation: 12 feet at Alki

This is a wonderful trail for looking at Puget Sound, the Olympic Mountains, and downtown Seattle. The trail is really a sidewalk alongside Elliott Bay and the Duwamish River with good access to several public parks. There are many nearby amenities, including food, fishing, and water access. Stop at the Seacrest Boat House for fishing information, aquarium displays, and quick lunches.

This trail is ideal for walks with family or out-of-town visitors. It is also popular with skaters and bicyclists on their way to Alki. The views are spectacular. The Olympic Mountains are so close, with what looks like only a small body of water separating the viewer from their snow-capped peaks. There is always a variety of boat traffic on Puget Sound and Elliott Bay. The trail offers perhaps the

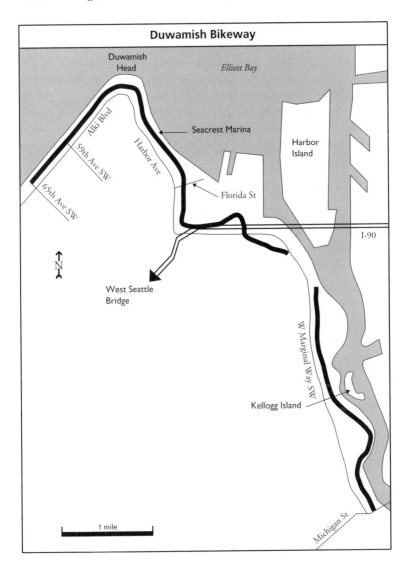

Duwamish Bikeway

best view of Seattle's skyline, with the Space Needle and Smith Tower acting as bookends for the numerous skyscrapers.

To get to the north end of the trail, take the Spokane Street bridge to the Harbor Avenue exit and go north to where Harbor Avenue turns west. This landform is called Duwamish Head because it is the headland next to the outflow of the Duwamish River. Follow Alki Boulevard west to 65th Avenue West. To get to the south end, take I-5 to the Michigan Street exit. Go west to West Marginal Way Southwest and look for the trail on the north side of Michigan Street.

The trail officially starts at 59th Avenue Southwest, where the route becomes separated from car traffic by a curb. Just south is a large park, popular with fishers, with a boat launch and restrooms. Farther south is Seacrest Marina, which has a large fishing dock, small fishing boats to rent, and a shop with fishing supplies and a

A family walks with Seattle in the background

soup-and-sandwich deli. South of Salty's Restaurant is public access at Terminal 5, operated by the Port of Seattle.

At Florida Street the trail ends, but you'll find a bike route along Florida Street to West Marginal Way Southwest. Go east on Florida Street to West Marginal Way Southwest and follow it under the West Seattle Freeway. There is a paved bike path on the south side of this street going under the freeway.

The rail-trail begins again at the entrance to Terminal 105 (big sign). The railroad line is still active, and the trail is wedged between the railroad and neighboring businesses. Though not particularly scenic here, the trail does provide a safe, nonmotorized route along a busy road with much truck traffic. At Kellogg Island, a wildlife sanctuary, there is public access and a park. Otherwise the trail parallels West Marginal Way Southwest and the railroad.

The City of Seattle plans to continue this trail south to Tukwila. Maybe someday there will be a completely separated paved trail all the way to Pacific at the south end of King County on this route. This trail is an example of how an active railroad right-of-way can be shared for nonmotorized use, providing the only route through an otherwise very developed area.

16 Foothills Trail

Pierce County Parks and Recreation

Endpoints: McMillin to South Prairie
Length: 10.8 miles
Surface: paved
Restrictions: 10 mph maximum speed
Original railroad: Chicago, Milwaukee and St. Paul Railroad
Location: Everett, Snohomish County
Latitude/longitude: N47° 8.38'/W122° 14.18'
Elevation: 130 feet at McMillin, 472 feet at Cascade Junction Road

The Foothills Trail starts in the Puyallup River valley and climbs into the foothills of the Cascade Mountains. It offers great views of Mount Rainier and the Carbon River and is a scenic route from Orting to South Prairie. It is a rural trail in an area that is quickly becoming urbanized.

To get to the north end, from SR 410 go south on SR 162 toward Orting. After about 3 miles, cross a bridge with a railroad bridge on your right. Turn right into the McMillin trailhead. There are restrooms and good parking at this location. To get to the east end, continue south and east on SR 162 past the town of South Prairie. Turn right on Cascade Junction Road and you will soon cross the trail. Park off the road and off of the trail.

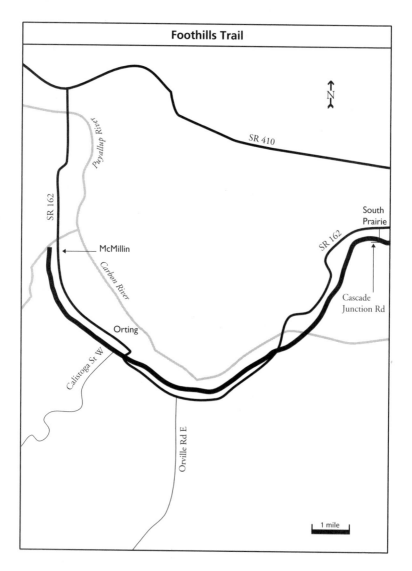

Heading toward Orting with a spectacular view of Mount Rainier

The trail begins at the McMillin trailhead. It goes south toward Orting, paralleling SR 162, and offers a great view of Mount Rainier. The trail is situated between Highway 162 and many new housing developments, a golf course, and a grade school.

In Orting the trail jogs around to go through the main town park with trees, shade, picnic tables, parking, food stores, and bathrooms. There used to be several tracks here, and you can see how the town grew up around the tracks. There is a grocery store nearby, and there are several restaurants.

Continuing south, you soon find yourself next to the Carbon River. There is a great rest spot with a picnic table right on the banks of the river. The trail stays close to the river for another 0.5 mile. Then it parallels and crosses over Highway 162. After crossing over the Carbon River on an old railroad bridge, it ends just after South Pioneer Way (Cascade Junction Road).

This was not an easy trail to build. When the trail was first proposed, many residents in the valley were opposed to its development. Since that time the valley has become mostly a suburban housing tract. Now the trail is seen as a wonderful amenity for the many people who live there. The trail is successful because of the hard work and diligence of the Foothills Trail Coalition, a local nonprofit organization.

The Foothills Trail is part of the Washington Cross-State Trail system. There are plans to extend this trail north to Puyallup, east to Buckley, and south to Carbanado.

17 Interurban Trail

Snohomish County Parks and Recreation

Endpoints: Edmonds to Everett
Length: 14.0 miles
Surface: paved
Restrictions: none
Original railroad: Interurban Railway
Location: Edmonds and Everett, Snohomish County
Latitude/longitude: N47° 47.61'/W122° 19.76'
Elevation: 290 feet at Edmonds, 553 feet high point, 363 feet at Pinehurst

This trail tries to retrace the route of the Interurban Railway that at one time operated between Tacoma and Bellingham, linking most of the communities that now are passed by I-5. This interurban line is the same one now used by the King County Interurban Trail and the Whatcom County Interurban Trail. The original route allows nonmotorized passage through a heavily urbanized and growing area.

To get to the south end in Edmonds, from I-5 take exit 179 (220th Street Southwest). Go west and turn south on SR 99. Turn east on 224th Street Southwest, south on 73rd Place Southwest, and east on 226th Place Southwest. To get to the north end, from I-5 take exit 189. Turn right onto Broadway and then soon left onto Beverly Boulevard and east onto Madison Street downhill to Commercial Avenue. Here is a small park called Interurban Park in the Pinehurst neighborhood of Everett.

Unfortunately, road development and many years of being abandoned mean that the trail does not always follow the original railroad right-of-way. Much of the right-of-way is owned by various electrical utilities that have built their substations right in the middle of the line. Sometimes the trail has been diverted around these obstacles. There are also some major road crossings, including I-5, that are passable but not the ideal routes for those seeking separation

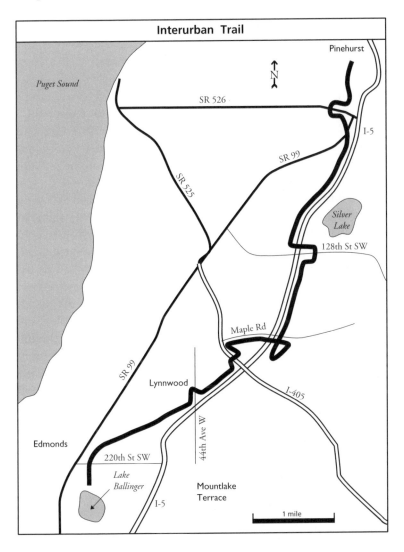

Interurban Trail

from cars. At some points the trail itself is shared by cars. But despite these difficulties, a detailed route winds through a heavily developed landscape and makes nonmotorized travel not only possible but also quite fun.

The various jurisdictions have tried to make it easier to help you find your way by using consistent trail route markings. You will have to look closely for them in some places, but they will point you in the right directions. Because the trail is close to both homes and business, this trail is a popular commuting and business route for people going to shop, school, or parks. Of course, it is also used for just taking walks or bike rides for relaxation.

Starting at the south end in Edmonds, the trail heads north alongside Hall Creek, which is hidden by vegetation. The pavement stops because there is a planned overpass for the busy 220th Street Southwest crossing. When you come to 220th Street Southwest, go to a crosswalk to cross; the traffic goes very fast up and down this steep road. Continuing north the trail becomes paved and leads up to 212th Street Southwest, where a detour is required off of the railroad grade. Head west on 212th Street Southwest to the crosswalk and go north along 63rd Avenue West and take the first right on 211th Street Southwest, which turns north and becomes 61st Avenue West. Turn right into a park on the north edge of the tennis courts. The paved path continues here and goes through some trees and comes out on the railroad right-of-way again.

At 54th Avenue West there is also a detour. Go north on 54th Avenue West to 208th Street Southwest. Go east one block and turn north on 53rd Avenue West a short way and look for the trail under the power lines. From here up to the park-and-ride the trail is away from roads and houses but approaches I-5. The trail skirts the edge of the Lynnwood park-and-ride lot, crosses the outbound bus lane, and curves around onto the south side sidewalk of 44th Avenue West, a main seven-lane arterial. At some time in the future there might be an overpass over 44th Avenue West. Until then, go north along 44th Avenue West to the intersection with 200th Street Southwest. Cross north across the crosswalk and follow 200th Street Southwest until you see an Interurban Trail sign on your right. The separated trail begins again here and climbs over a large overpass crossing SR 524.

Strolling near Alderwood Mall

After the overpass the trail is wedged between I-5 and the frontage road. At the end of a long straightaway you pass under Alderwood Mall Boulevard through a wide tunnel. The trail goes onto some side dead-end roads and back to a separated trail several times before coming out on Ash Way. Turn right on Maple Road and begin to climb up and over I-5. This is a steep climb, but it enables you to get over the freeway. Turn right on Butternut Road and take the first right onto the restart of the trail, which curls back under Maple Road.

The trail is right next to the freeway, separated by grass and a chain link fence. It climbs uphill going north and then turns east to Meadow Road. Turn left (north) on Meadow Road and cross 164th Street Southwest. At 160th Street Southwest turn left and the trail begins again on the north side of 160th Street Southwest.

From here there is a very long stretch where the trail is separated from road traffic. It climbs up a long hill and then down the other side. Just before 128th Street Southwest it turns east and enters the roadway at 130th Place Southwest. From here the route follows 130th Place Southwest east, which turns north and becomes 3rd Avenue Southeast. Turn left onto 128th Street Southwest (a very busy arterial) and climb up and over I-5 using the sidewalk or roadway if you are bicycling. Once over I-5, take the first right, where the separated trail begins again. After another section parallel to the freeway on the west side, the trail turns west and heads directly into West Mall Drive, a private road. Keep to the right, either in the bike lane or on the sidewalk. Cross Southeast Everett Mall Way and continue 0.25 mile, which leads you directly into the trail.

In 0.5 mile the trail ends at 84th Street Southeast. Turn left on 84th Street Southeast and right on 7th Avenue Southeast. Take an immediate right onto East Casino Road, which takes you under SR 526. Keep right and enter a short trail segment that comes out at Pinkerton Avenue Southeast. *Caution:* The trail takes a steep 9 percent drop with a tight corner at the bottom.

From this point north the trail is away from the busy highways and in the backyards of numerous homes. Cross Beverly Boulevard with a light and continue north to Madison Street, the current northern terminus in the Pinehurst neighborhood of Everett. Here there is a small park called Interurban Park celebrating the old rail line.

Although not a continuous path like most rail-trails, the trail segments are linked by a common set of signs pointing the way through several cities in Snohomish County. There are plans to connect the north end of the trail with the Lowell Snohomish Trail. There are also plans to continue this trail south to 85th Street in Seattle. This would make it a very long urban and suburban trail through a very congested and growing area.

18 Issaquah Creek Trail

King County Parks

Endpoints: High Point to Issaquah
Length: 2.0 miles
Surface: hard-packed gravel
Restrictions: no camping
Original railroad: Seattle, Lake Shore & Eastern Railroad, built 1890, abandoned 1974
Location: High Point, 2 miles east of Issaquah, King County
Latitude/longitude: N47° 31.93'/W121° 58.81'
Elevation: 475 feet at High Point, 257 feet near Issaquah

This rail-trail offers an easy hike and bike route in a beautiful forest alongside Issaquah Creek. Though very close to an urban community and the I-90 freeway, it is a safe, secluded, tree-lined rail-trail. The trail is a wonderful place to unwind after work, and in the hot summer its cover of trees keeps it cool. It is great for walking, mountain biking, and horseback riding. It is also much less crowded than the Tiger Mountain trailhead. To get to the east trailhead, take I-90 to exit 22 (High Point) and turn north under the freeway just past the interchange to a parking area west of the frontage road. Metro Bus 210 has a stop here.

This rail-trail parallels I-90 just east of Issaquah. The trail connects

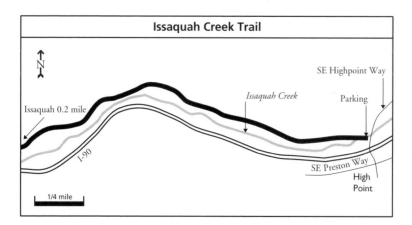

Cyclists heading uphill in the summer

to the west with Issaquah. However, you must leave the railway grade and duck under the freeway where Issaquah Creek goes under I-90. In the future there will be a large freeway overpass system and the trail will be routed across the creek. Going east from High Point there is a faint trail between the creek and the freeway fence all the way to the Preston–Snoqualmie Trail. King County Parks has plans to develop the Issaquah Creek Trail into a paved trail connecting west to the planned East Lake Sammamish Trail and the existing western terminus of the Preston–Snoqualmie Trail.

19 King County Interurban Trail

King County Parks, City of Kent Parks and Recreation Department

Endpoints: Tukwila to Pacific
Length: 15.0 miles
Surface: asphalt
Restrictions: open in daylight only
Original railroad: Seattle Tacoma Interurban Railway, abandoned 1929
Location: Tukwila, Kent, Auburn, Algona, and Pacific, King County
Latitude/longitude: N47° 27.66'/W122° 14.54'
Elevation: 23 feet

Cutting through the midst of a forest of warehouses in the Kent Valley is a path of green. The King County Interurban Trail follows the route of the old interurban railroad that once connected the urban centers of western Washington. Where the route once served as a major transportation corridor through farmland, it now serves as a major recreation and nonmotorized transportation route through industrial development. This rail-trail was made possible because Puget Power and Light purchased the railroad right-of-way for a high-voltage power line that runs the entire trail length.

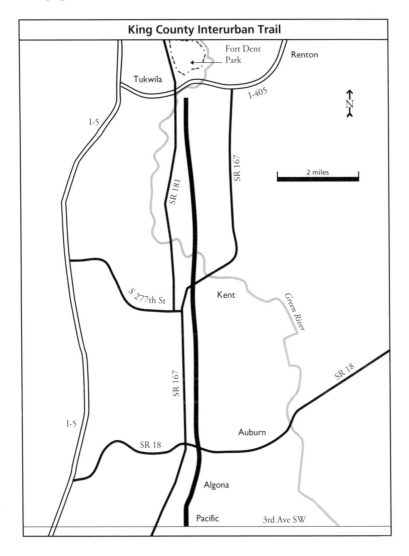

King County Interurban Trail

To get to the north end of the trail, take I-5 to I-405 and take Interurban Boulevard (SR 181) south one block. Turn east on South Longacres Way and go east one block. The trail heads south from here. The trail north goes under I-405 and ends at Grady Way. To get to the south end, take SR 169 south to exit on Ellingson Road. Turn right (south) on Tacoma Boulevard North. Go south and turn left on 3rd Avenue Southwest. You will cross the trail in three blocks.

This rail-trail offers a long route for a quiet bike ride or walk away from busy streets, with views of Mount Rainier and, along the southern half, what is left of the green farmlands of the Kent Valley. It is one of the oldest rail-trails in Washington State (parts of it opened in 1972), and it exemplifies how preserving a railroad right-of-way for a trail also preserves greenspace. Since the construction of this trail, most of the Kent Valley has been taken over by major warehouse buildings, but this trail preserves a strip of green right down the middle of the valley. It also preserves small wetland strips and provides food and shelter for a variety of animals, including birds, rabbits, frogs, and numerous insects.

The trail is also popular with wheelchair users, particularly wheelchair racers, who train here regularly. These athletes have a special need for long stretches of paved surface safe from motor vehicle traffic. One local company makes special racing chairs that you may see being used on the trail.

Although there are areas with concrete tilt-up buildings on both sides, the trail is somewhat quiet because it is isolated from most motorized traffic by those buildings. The route parallels the Union Pacific's active main line, which comes as close as 30 feet at times. There is no real danger because sufficient green marshes exist to keep people from the tracks, and the passing trains remind trail users that trains once ran where they now walk, run, and bicycle. The trail is popular with those who work in the Kent Valley. Many use the trail for their commute and even more use it for daytime exercise.

Starting from the north end, the trail winds alongside the very large power transmission towers. On the west are the backs of large warehouses. On the east is a border of green and then the main-line railroad tracks with an occasional train. The trail goes 5 miles south with little interruption until it passes under SR 167 and skirts the

The greenbelt is preserved by the trail north of Auburn.

east side of the Kent Uplands Playfield. The old downtown of Kent is three blocks east. There you can find food, shops, and baseball diamonds. A farmers' market is held off Smith Street on second Saturdays during the summer.

The rail-trail winds west to cross Willis Street, a main east–west arterial through Kent. It then regains the railroad grade and goes south 1.0 mile to a bridge over the Green River. There is a small park just north of this bridge, with picnic tables adjacent to the river. The bridge provides a good view of the water and the trains crossing the railroad trestle only 100 feet to the west.

Continuing south, the trail crosses two railroad spurs to large automobile storage areas. It then crosses 74th Avenue South and goes across a smaller bridge over a wetland area. There are a few parking spaces just north across 74th Avenue South.

The trail south is separated from most of the industrial build-ings and offers views of working farms, old barns, occasionally Mount Rainier, and airplanes landing at the Auburn Airport. At mile 12.0 is the Auburn trailhead on Northwest 15th Street, with parking for about twenty cars. At mile 14.5 cross First Avenue North in Algona, where you can find a restaurant and mini-mart near the trail and parking for trail users. The southern terminus of the trail is at mile 15.0 in the town of Pacific at Third Avenue Southwest near Highway 167, with parking for ten vehicles. The railroad grade south of here lies in Pierce County and has not been developed yet.

20 Lake Wilderness Trail

King County Parks

Endpoints: Maple Valley to Summit
Length: 3.9 miles
Surface: hard-packed dirt and loose gravel
Restrictions: none
Original railroad: Columbia and Puget Sound Railway
Location: Maple Valley, King County
Latitude/longitude: N47° 24.29'/W122° 2.41'
Elevation: 324 feet at Maple Valley, 577 feet at SR 516

This is a short section of what will someday be a longer trail running from Maple Valley to the Green River. The current open section extends from Lake Wilderness County Park north to Maple Valley and south to Summit. An interesting feature of this trail is that the dirt surface is very black, the result of years of coal falling off the coal trains from Black Diamond.

To get to the west end, from SR 169 just before Maple Valley turn off into a gravel parking area on the east side of the road. Take the northern gravel trail, the Cedar River Trail, across the Cedar River. At about 0.5 mile watch for a sign on the right pointing uphill to the Lake Wilderness Trail. To get to the south end of the trail continue south on SR 169 to where it crosses SR 516. Turn west on SR 516, go one block and look for the trail on the right.

This trail generally is in the shade of deciduous trees lining it on both sides until just before the southern end. It climbs gently through a draw and passes through three short culverts and tunnels. There are not many views until you reach Lake Wilderness County Park, and even there you have to peer through the trees to see the lake. There is access to the park at the north end of the lake via an unmarked side trail. The county park has water access, restrooms, picnic areas, a conference building, and other amenities.

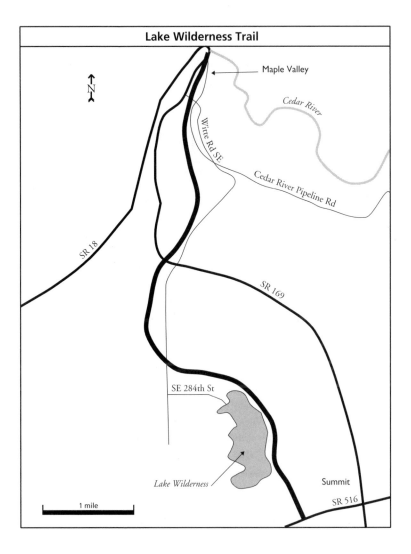

Lake Wilderness Trail

Running the dog near Lake Wilderness

There is also an arboretum developed by the South King County Arboretum Foundation. It includes a wonderful series of trails that crisscross the rail-trail in deep, dark woods.

As the trail passes along the south end of the lake it passes through a housing development with large homes and a private waterfront beach. Please stay on the trail. From here south is a straight trail that eases off in grade and ends at SR 516 between two commercial shopping areas.

The name "Lake Wilderness County Park" may seem incongruous today with all the growth in the area. Although at one time this county park may have been viewed as wilderness, new housing encroaches on the lake. But it is the foresight to create these parks and trails before the population reaches them that makes living nearby so attractive.

King County plans to extend this trail south to Black Diamond and eventually to Flaming Geyser State Park.

22 Northwest Timber Trail

Department of Natural Resources

Endpoints: Tiger Summit trailhead to Road 7500
Length: 2.0 miles
Surface: dirt
Restrictions: no horses, closed October through April
Original railroad: Preston Railroad
Location: Preston, King County
Latitude/longitude: N47° 28.05'/W121° 55.76'
Elevation: 1393 feet

This rough, woodsy trail follows an old railroad grade as much as possible. It is built in the dark forest on the east side of Tiger Mountain State Forest. There are no views, but there are a few really big trees hidden along the trail near a steep creek crossing. It is an out-and-back trail, although you can link up with the Preston Railroad Trail to make a loop. It is very popular with mountain bicyclists, but because of the poor soil conditions it is a difficult trail for beginners.

To get to the trailhead, take SR 18 to Tiger Summit. If the parking lot next to the road still exists, take the eastside Road 7500 about 200 yards and look on the right for a small opening in the woods with a trail. There is also another formal trailhead on the Poo Poo Point Road. From this "new" trailhead take the Iverson Railroad Crossover trail going east to find the start of the trail on the east side of Road 7500.

The trail was designed to not be too steep but to wander through the woods. It passes through several large alder groves, skirts a hillside, and comes to the creek crossing. Here is a high bridge across a very narrow but deep creek. A bit further are two very large trees hidden in the woods downhill from the trail. Most people will never find them because the trees next to the trail block the sight of them.

The trail climbs, and then after a steep side slope comes to the railroad grade. It is smooth sailing with a slight downhill to Road 7500. You can get a good view to the northeast from this point before you head back.

21 Myrtle Edwards Park Trail

City of Seattle Engineering Department

Endpoints: West Galer Street to Broad Street
Length: 1.5 miles
Surface: 8- to 10-foot-wide asphalt
Restrictions: separate paths for pedestrians and wheeled vehicles, pet scoop law
Original railroad: Seattle, Lake Shore & Eastern Railroad
Location: Seattle, King County
Latitude/longitude: N47° 37.08'/W122° 21.50'
Elevation: 19 feet

This trail is situated at the water's edge in the City of Seattle, with a stunning view across Puget Sound to the Olympic Mountains. It is so close to downtown that many runners pass through Myrtle Edwards Park during their lunch hour. There is a strange contrast in hearing the sounds of the city and the lap of the waves against the breakwater, seeing the city skyline and smelling the salty air off the seawater.

This trail is very popular with walkers and runners, both visitors and residents. It is also a major commuting route for bicyclists on their way to work downtown. The separate walking and wheeled-vehicle paths help add capacity, which is especially useful during the busy summer.

To reach the southern access, go to Alaskan Way on the Seattle waterfront and go north to Broad Street. The park entrance is at the intersection of Broad Street and Alaskan Way. You need to go around the trolley maintenance building to see the park. To reach the north access, take Elliott Avenue West to West Galer Street and turn west toward the water. The right lane is marked to the Pier 89 public fishing pier. Turn left (south) into the marked parking area. There is good parking at both ends of the trail.

The trail starts at the south end near the trolley maintenance shops. The trolley is a recent addition to the Seattle waterfront and runs south to Pioneer Square. The trail is actually two pathways: one for bicycles and one for pedestrians. The pedestrian path is

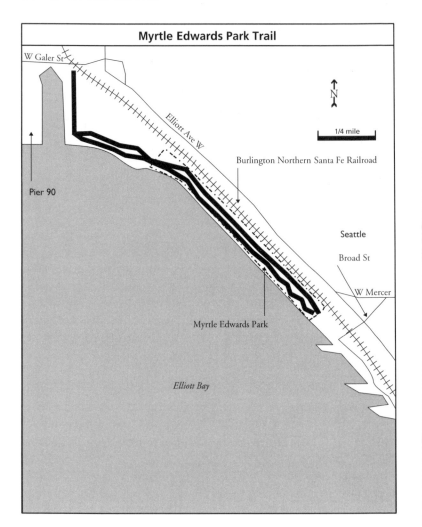

Myrtle Edwards Park Trail

W Galer St

Elliott Ave W

N

1/4 mile

Burlington Northern Santa Fe Railroad

Pier 90

Seattle

Broad St

W Mercer

Myrtle Edwards Park

Elliott Bay

for both the Sea-Tac and Boeing fields. There is a variety of
traffic on Elliott Bay, including cruise liners, commercial ships, t
the ever-present ferries, and the occasional Coast Guard icebre
or military vessel.

Approximately 1 mile from the south end is a large, mo
public fishing dock with a bait-and-tackle shop open in the s
mertime. You can catch dinner off the dock, and many peopl
Near the north end of the park is a par course, an exercise cc
running along the park. For those more interested in views
exercise, there are many park benches along the route and a
views.

Although commonly called Myrtle Edwards Park, the nor
part of the park is Port of Seattle property and is called Elliot
Park. This park was opened in 1975.

At the north end, the trail leaves the waterfront and pro
alongside a parking area. It connects with the Terminal 91 Bik
to the north, accessed by crossing at West Galer Street. The Ter
91 Bike Trail passes through the main BNSF switchyard and
out on 20th Avenue West. At the south end of Myrtle Edwards
there is a connection with the sidewalk system along the wat
and Alaskan Way, and perhaps someday there will be a conr
with the Seattle Waterfront Path.

Looking south toward downtown Seattle

closer to the water and passes various pieces of public art. Just over
the fence to the east is an active Burlington Northern switchyard,
which holds cars serving the large grain terminal. This terminal has
an interpretive sign next to the trail explaining its operation.

This trail provides views in all directions. To the south you see
the towering Seattle skyline, the busy waterfront, and the huge cranes
of the port facilities. To the west you look across Elliott Bay to Alki
and beyond to the Olympic Mountains. To the north you see the
steep bluffs of Magnolia. Overhead is a constant stream of planes

The author was responsible for laying out the route for this trail through the rugged terrain with Walt Shostak of the Backcountry Bicycle Trails Club (BBTC). Much of the development and maintenance work on this trail was completed by the BBTC.

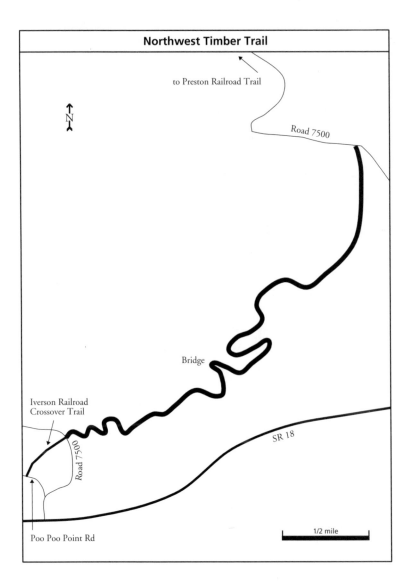

Northwest Timber Trail

Two intrepid hikers by the waterfall

23 Preston Railroad Trail

Department of Natural Resources

Endpoints: Crossover Road 5500 to Main Tiger Mountain Road 4000
Length: 5.0 miles
Surface: dirt
Restrictions: no horses, closed October through April
Original railroad: Preston Railroad, abandoned 1920s
Location: Tiger Mountain State Forest, King County
Latitude/longitude: N47° 29.80'/W121° 55.55'
Elevation: 1604 feet at Road 5500, 2515 feet at Road 4000

High on the east side of Tiger Mountain is a wonderful rail-trail built on an old logging railroad grade. The existence of the railroad grade provides a strong foundation for a mountain bike trail. It also made the construction of this trail far easier than that of other trails. The entire trail is in deep woods, which keep it cool in the summer and protect people from gentle rains.

To get to the higher end of the trail, take SR 18 to Tiger Summit and drive into the main parking area. There is a trail that goes north

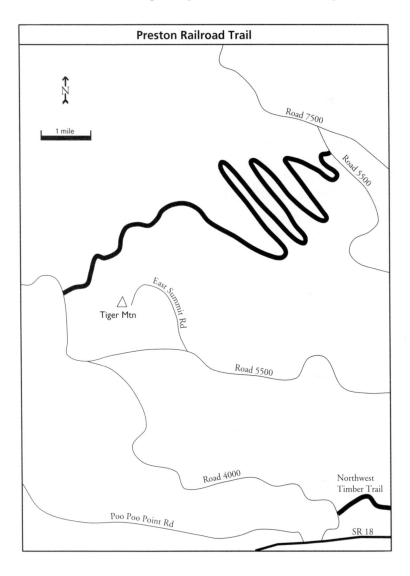

Happy cyclists deep in the woods

and then east that connects to the main Tiger Mountain Road 4000 2.5 miles to the first intersection. Turn left and proceed 0.5 mile to a low spot in the road to the right. The trail is to the right, at the base of the steep hill. To get to the lower end, take the Northwest Timber Trail to the eastside Road 7500. Follow the eastside road northeast 4.2 miles to a switchback. Turn uphill on the Crossover Road 5500 for 300 feet and look for the trail entrance on the uphill side. It is much easier to climb the road than the trail because the road, although steeper, is smooth and hardpacked.

This is an easy hiking trail but definitely an intermediate mountain bike trail. The soil is very poor, and numerous springs play havoc with the trail surface. Be prepared to get muddy almost any time of the year.

This trail was built by volunteers through the coordination of the Backcountry Bicycle Trails Club (BBTC). The route was laid out by the author and members of the BBTC. It is an example of a user group working cooperatively with the managing agency and other user groups to create a popular trail.

24 Preston—Snoqualmie Trail

King County Parks

Endpoints: Preston to Snoqualmie Falls overlook
Length: 6.2 miles
Surface: asphalt with gravel switchbacks
Restrictions: 15-mph speed limit, dogs on leash
Original railroad: Seattle, Lake Shore & Eastern Railroad, built 1890, abandoned 1974, trail opened 1978
Location: Preston, King County
Latitude/longitude: N47° 31.32'/W121° 55.94'
Elevation: 496 feet at Preston Trailhead, 455 feet at trail end

This paved rail-trail wanders along through deep woods and emerges with a spectacular view of Snoqualmie Falls. Most of the trail is in second-growth timber with deciduous trees. This makes it cool in the summer and allows views during the winter. Part of the trail was opened in 1978, yet it still does not receive a great deal of use.

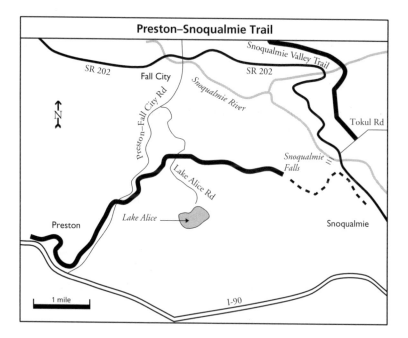

Mount Si, viewed from the east end of the trail

The trail is good for walking any time of year. The pavement ensures dry feet, even in the rain, and it is almost never covered with snow. It also makes a good bike ride, although one section of gravel switchbacks presents a challenge even for the skilled mountain bike rider. Equestrians are welcome, although the paved surface may not be to their liking.

To get to the main trailhead at the western end, take exit 22 (Preston) from I-90 and head north across the freeway. Turn immediately right on the Preston–Fall City Road for two blocks and turn left on SE 87th Place. There is a small parking lot for seven cars.

One part of the trail continues west from the trailhead 0.9 mile through an industrial area and then ends. Going east, the trail goes above the town of Preston, an old mill town. It traverses the hillside north of town, where there is a wide path down to the town site and to Preston County Park. The trail continues along a steep hillside until it comes to where there used to be a tremendous trestle across the valley of the Raging River. It descends very steeply to the Preston–Fall City Road and then climbs gravel switchbacks up to the original grade. *Caution:* Be very careful going downhill on this section because the trail ends abruptly at the highway with no warning. Carefully cross the highway and stay on the water side of the jersey barriers placed along the road until you get to the gravel switchbacks.

At the top of the switchbacks is a bench, with views back across the valley.

At 3.5 miles from the Preston trailhead you'll find a parking area and trailhead at Lake Alice Road; then the trail continues to a beautiful overlook of Snoqualmie Falls at 5.3 miles from the trail-head. Although you are about 2 miles away, you can see the falls and the lodge hanging over the lip, and in the spring you can hear the thunder of the cascading water.

From the western terminus there is no formal trail heading west. Bicyclists can use the frontage road to High Point to connect with the Issaquah Creek Trail. Hikers can follow the faint trail along the freeway fence that eventually leads to the Issaquah Creek Trail. In the future this trail will continue east and connect with the Sno-qualmie Centennial Corridor Trail. It will pass over two major trestles and have a spectacular view of Snoqualmie Falls.

25 Seattle Waterfront Pathway

City of Seattle Engineering Department

Endpoints: Bell Street to Royal Brougham Way
Length: 1.5 miles
Surface: asphalt
Restrictions: no horses
Original railroad: Seattle, Lake Shore & Eastern Railroad; trail opened 1990
Location: Seattle waterfront, King County
Latitude/longitude: N47° 36.71'/W122° 20.90'
Elevation: 40 feet

This urban rail-trail was created to improve pedestrian movement in the waterfront area of Seattle. For years the railroad tracks and the Alaskan Way Viaduct were a barrier to pedestrians passing from downtown Seattle to the waterfront. The City of Seattle reclaimed one of its most valuable assets, the waterfront area, and this trail improves the nonmotorized access. The trail was developed between a new trolley system and the Alaskan Way Viaduct, creating a nonmotorized corridor in a heavily used area of the city.

To reach the north end of the trail, from Alaskan Way turn east across the trolley line tracks at Bell Street, near the World Trade Center. The rail-trail lies immediately east of the trolley tracks. To get to the south end, take Alaskan Way south to Royal Brougham Way, where the trail begins on the east side of the tracks and heads north.

There are many interesting places to visit along this route and numerous access points. This is a pedestrian route to get to the Pike Place Market, perched high on the hillside. The market has a variety of fresh food and fish vendors, small shops, and restaurants. The trail, used mostly by pedestrians and runners, is also appropriate for low-speed cyclists trying to avoid narrow and busy Alaskan Way.

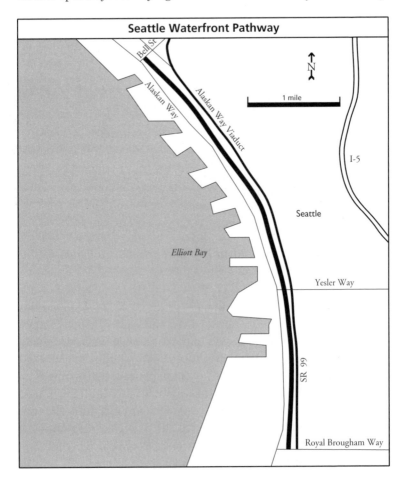

The Seattle waterfront and trolley squeeze the trail next to the viaduct.

Toward the south end of the trail across Alaskan Way are the Washington Street Public Boat Landing and a small park. Farther north is the Washington State ferry terminal, with ferries to Bainbridge Island and Bremerton. There are trolley stations every two blocks; you can take a trolley to return to your starting point.

The trail currently ends at the north end at Bell Street, where you must cross Alaskan Way to the west side to get to Myrtle Edwards Park to the north. The City of Seattle plans to continue this rail-trail along Alaskan Way, then west across the Duwamish River and Harbor Island to connect with the Duwamish Trail.

26 Snohomish—Arlington Centennial Trail

Snohomish County Parks and Recreation

Endpoints: Snohomish to Lake Stevens
Length: 5.75 miles
Surface: asphalt
Restrictions: none
Original railroad: Seattle, Lake Shore & Eastern Railroad
Location: Snohomish to Edgecomb, Snohomish County
Latitude/longitude: N47° 55.59'/W122° 4.80'
Elevation: 71 feet at Snohomish, 207 feet at 20th Street Northeast

This is a wonderful rail-trail in the rural but growing part of Snohomish County. It provides a scenic route through an agricultural and forested section of the county that is fast becoming suburban. There is a separate horse path for most of the length.

To get to the south trailhead, take SR 2 to the Snohomish exit. Turn left onto Second Street and left (north) on Maple Avenue. Going north, the rail-trail is on the right, about 1 mile north of town where Pine Avenue crosses. You can park along Maple Avenue. There is a bike shop, Centennial Bikes, in the indoor soccer arena just south of here. There is a trailhead 1.5 miles further north, the Pilchuck Trailhead, with a large gravel parking area and signs. The northern terminus of the paved portion of the trail is at 20th Street Northeast just east of Lake Stevens. The trail north of here is undeveloped, and there is no public parking where the trail intersects roads.

The trail starts in Snohomish, a long-time agricultural town that recently has seen tremendous growth. The old downtown area has many antique and food stores and is a wonderful place to start or end a trail journey. The trail starts at the north end of town alongside Maple Avenue. It parallels the Snohomish–Machias Road through lowland farm areas next to the Pilchuck River. At Machias there is a great trailhead and picnic area with toilets and a picnic spot.

At about 3.25 miles is the Machias Trailhead. This has restrooms, a covered picnic area, and a concession during the summer with food and drinks. This is the best place to stop for a rest, even if you are going farther north, because there are no facilities north of here. The trail ends at 20th Street Northeast near Lake Stevens.

This trail is the result of the efforts of the Snohomish–Arlington Centennial Trail Coalition, a citizens' group that provided tremendous

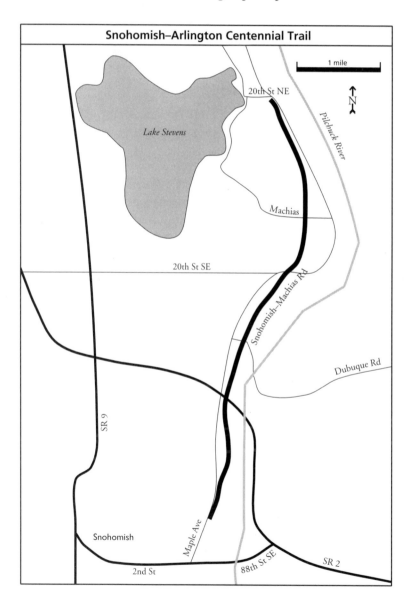

A group of equestrians enjoying a shaded ride

support to the Snohomish County Parks Department. There are plans for this trail to continue to Edgecomb, just south of Arlington. The City of Arlington plans to extend a trail through the city and connect it to this trail. The Snohomish Parks Department plans to continue the trail north of Arlington to the Skagit County line and east to Darrington. There are also plans to connect this trail south through Monroe to the Snoqualmie Valley Trail in King County.

27 Snoqualmie Centennial Corridor Trail

City of Snoqualmie

Endpoints: Southeast Northern Street to Snoqualmie River
Length: 0.5 mile
Surface: asphalt
Restrictions: no horses; dogs must be on leash
Original railroad: Seattle, Lake Shore & Eastern Railroad, built 1890, trail opened 1989
Location: Snoqualmie, King County
Latitude/longitude: N47° 31.91'/W121° 49.66'
Elevation: 407 feet at Snoqualmie

This is a rail-trail for steam railroad fans. The trail is constructed alongside an active railroad, with scenic train excursions operated by the Snoqualmie and Puget Sound Railway out to the Snoqualmie Falls. This nonprofit group has restored the train depot, steam engines, and many railroad cars, although they have many more rusting alongside the trail. Excursion trains run on summer weekends and for Halloween and Christmas. This trail also serves as a safe route for nonmotorized use between Snoqualmie and Snoqualmie Falls, avoiding the narrow and busy Highway 202 and a connection to the Snoqualmie Ridge Parkway Trail.

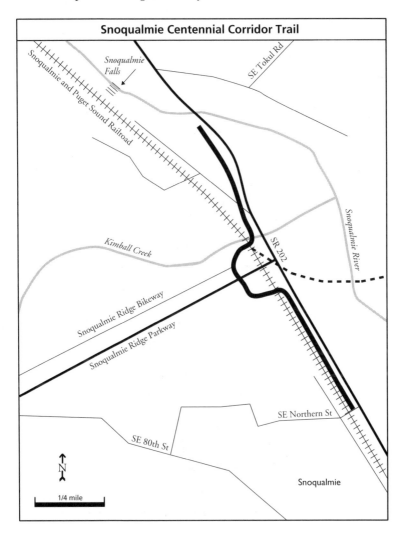

The Seattle, Lake Shore & Eastern Railroad was built by Daniel Gilman, one of the partners who built the railroad route along which the Burke–Gilman Trail is now located. This railroad originally opened from Seattle as far as Snoqualmie on the Fourth of July in 1890.

To get to the trail, take I-90 to exit 31 and follow SR 202 through North Bend to the center of Snoqualmie. Park just west of the railway station on the south side of the railroad tracks. The trail starts farther west at Southeast Northern Street.

The trail crosses Kimball Creek on a railroad flatcar bridge. There is also a narrow dirt path that goes north under SR 202 and leads to the Snoqualmie River, where there is a great view of Mount Si. Just north is the intersection with the Snoqualmie Parkway Trail, which connects to I-90. The trail ends at the intersection of SR 202 and the Snoqualmie River. Stay on the sidewalk across the bridge, then walk through a parking area to get to Snoqualmie Falls. You'll also find access to the Snoqualmie Valley Trail by going north on Southeast Tokul Road for 0.5 mile.

The trail connects to the east with a sidewalk system on the south side of the parking lot that goes to the Snoqualmie Railway Station. In the future, King County Parks plans to extend its Preston–Snoqualmie Trail up to Snoqualmie Falls and connect with the western terminus of this trail.

A passenger car passes close by the trail.

28 Snoqualmie Valley Trail

King County Parks

Endpoints: Duvall to Southeast Tokul Road
Length: 21.5 miles
Surface: gravel and dirt
Restrictions: none
Original railroad: Chicago, Milwaukee, St. Paul, and Pacific Railroad
Location: Duvall and Carnation, King County
Latitude/longitude: N47° 44.39'/W121° 59.25'
Elevation: 81 feet at Duvall, 501 feet at Southeast Tokul Road

This is a wonderful trail through lush forests and the lowland farms along the east side of the Carnation Valley. The trail passes through the lowlands and climbs high enough to provide great views of the valley. It is an ideal place for equestrians, mountain bikers, hikers, bird watchers, and view seekers. It is very close to the urban Seattle area yet is in a truly rural setting.

To get to the north end of the trail, take SR 203 to Duvall. South of the bridge over the Snoqualmie River is an access road to the trail. To get to the south end, take SR 202 to Snoqualmie Falls. Turn north on Southeast Tokul Road 0.5 mile to a large culvert over the trail. Take the next side road to the right and look for a small trail down to the grade.

The best access to the trail is in Carnation. This gives you the choice of going 9.7 miles south or 11.8 miles north one way. Take exit 22 from I-90, turn left (north) across the freeway, and turn right on the Preston–Fall City Road to Fall City. From Fall City, cross over the Snoqualmie River, turn left (northwest) on SR 203, and go 5 miles to Carnation. In the center of Carnation turn right on Entwhistle Street, go right (east) four blocks to Milwaukee Avenue, and park at Nick Loutsis Park.

Starting at Carnation, the trail begins at Nick Loutsis Park and heads south across the Tolt River Bridge. This is a very long bridge over the wide floodplain area of the Tolt River, one of the water sources for Seattle. The trail passes behind Tolt High School and heads up and into the woods.

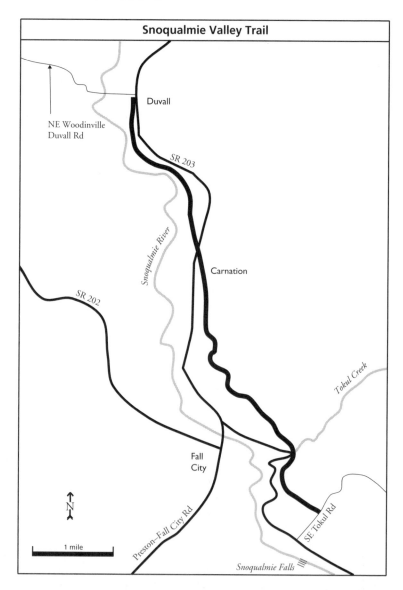

Snoqualmie Valley Trail

Duvall

NE Woodinville
Duvall Rd

SR 203

Snoqualmie River

SR 202

Carnation

Tokul Creek

Fall
City

N

1 mile

Preston–Fall City Rd

SE Tokul Rd

Snoqualmie Falls

At 1.8 miles is a bridge over Griffin Creek with a beautiful view of the wide valley below. The trail is in second-growth woods, with mostly deciduous trees covering the trail. Gradually the trail rounds a corner above Fall City, and through the trees you can see Fall City and Tiger Mountain in the distance. The trail east continues for

3.3 miles across the spectacular Tokul Creek Bridge and ends at an underpass of Southeast Tokul Road. This is 0.5 mile from the Snoqualmie Falls overlook.

Going north from Carnation the trail stays in the flat valley. Occasionally the Snoqualmie River meanders next to the trail grade. There are active farms and cattle ranches on both sides of the trail, and because the trail is elevated 10 feet above the valley floor, there is a good view.

In some places the fields are owned by the Department of Wildlife and are used for hunting in season. The access points have good parking areas near Stillwater, but you must have a Department of Wildlife Conservation license if you park a motor vehicle there. Because the railroad owned a 100-foot-wide right of way, there is a buffer of trees along this route between the trail and the surrounding farms. The trail currently ends at the south edge of the growing community of Duvall, which has shops, grocery stores, and restaurants.

In the future, this trail will continue north 3 miles to the Snohomish County line, where Snohomish County plans to continue it to

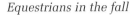

Equestrians in the fall

Monroe. To the south, the trail will someday connect with the Upper Snoqualmie Trail, the Snoqualmie Centennial Corridor Trail, and the Preston–Snoqualmie Trail.

29 South Ship Canal Trail

City of Seattle

Endpoints: Fremont Bridge to 6th Avenue West
Length: 0.5 mile
Surface: asphalt
Restrictions: no horses; dogs must be on leash
Original railroad: Seattle, Lake Shore & Eastern Railroad, built 1890, trail opened 1989
Location: Snoqualmie, King County
Latitude/longitude: N47° 38.83'/W122° 20.99'
Elevation: 17 feet at Fremont Bridge

This popular urban trail parallels the scenic ship canal built to move boats between Lake Washington, Lake Union, and Puget Sound. It is right next to the water, separated by a row of old cottonwood trees. The trail provides a safe, flat transportation and recreation

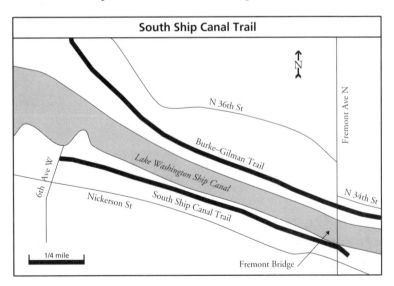

South Ship Canal Trail

A boat passing through the canal next to the trail

route on the south side of the ship canal, avoiding the very busy arterial one block south. It is heavily used by the students and staff of Seattle Pacific University, located adjacent to the trail.

To get to the east end, from the south side of the Fremont Bridge turn into the gravel parking area on the south side of Westlake Avenue, just east of the Fremont Bridge. The trail begins under the bridge in the railroad tunnel. To get to the west end, take Nickerson Avenue to 6th Avenue West and turn right. Go down the hill one block, and the trail begins on your right (east).

This is a great place to walk and to watch the boat traffic through the locks. It is a very popular commuting route for students and those living east of Seattle Pacific University. You can connect to the Burke–Gilman Trail by crossing over the Fremont Bridge and turning right on the first street.

The City of Seattle has plans to extend this trail west under the Ballard Bridge and connect it with popular bike routes going to the Locks, Discovery Park, and downtown via the Pier 91 Bikeway.

30 Upper Snoqualmie Valley Trail

King County Parks

Endpoints: Mill Pond Road to Rattlesnake Lake
Length: 9.0 miles
Surface: gravel
Restrictions: dogs on leash
Original railroad: Chicago, Milwaukee and St. Paul Railroad
Location: North Bend, King County
Latitude/longitude: N47° 31.79'/W121° 48.41'
Elevation: 405 feet at Mill Pond Road, 910 feet at Rattlesnake Lake

This trail is built on the same railroad line, the Milwaukee Road, as the Snoqualmie Valley Trail, which goes from Duvall to Tokul Road. It connects Snoqualmie and North Bend with Rattlesnake Lake and provides a safe, quiet, and scenic passageway to the lake.

The west end of this trail was not easily accessible at the time this trail was researched. There may be a temporary stairway attached to the bridge abutment, but it won't be good for bicycling or horseback riding. To get to the westernmost accessible point, take SR 522 to Snoqualmie, turn north on Meadowbrook Way SE, and then turn east on SE Park Street. Go about 0.25 mile and turn into the entrance to a golf course. You will see the trail running through the golf course. You can park on the trail between the signs marking the trail. If you are planning to go up to Rattlesnake Lake, the best starting point is in North Bend. In downtown North Bend, go north on Ballarat Avenue North three blocks and turn into the parking lot just north of the Two Rivers School. To get to the trailhead at Rattlesnake Lake, from I-90 take exit 32 (436th Avenue Southeast) and go 3 miles south to the parking area at Rattlesnake Lake. Note that cars will be towed if left after dark at the Rattlesnake Lake parking lot.

Starting at the west end, this trail crosses the Snoqualmie River and then right through the middle of a golf course. High cyclone fences protect the trail users. It then passes by the several farmland areas, including one owned by King County that may someday become a regional park (Three Rivers Park). It crosses the South Fork of the Snoqualmie River and enters North Bend. Where the trail

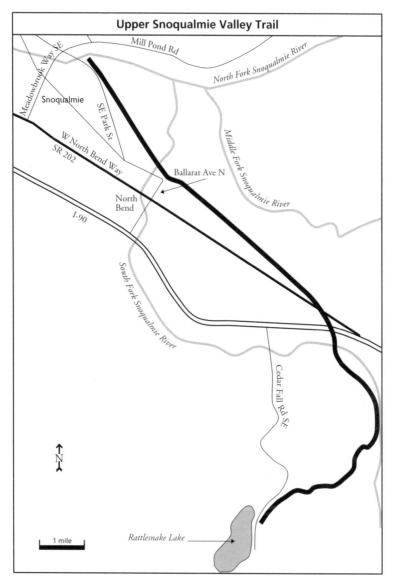

Upper Snoqualmie Valley Trail

crosses Ballarat Avenue North, it is three blocks north of the main street in North Bend, with shops, a grocery, and a bakery. There is also good parking here at the Two Rivers School area.

Continuing east, the trail crosses North Bend Boulevard under I-90 and then begins the climb to Rattlesnake Lake. Here the trail is

A man and his dog heading uphill near Rattlesnake Lake

in deep woods and shade, making it cool year-round. There are some views of the South Fork Snoqualmie River far below, and then the trail winds around the steep hills before the grade eases, approaching Rattlesnake Lake.

The development of a parking area and roads by the City of Seattle Water Department destroyed the old railroad grade near Rattlesnake Lake. Instead it is a wandering maze of old roads, new gravel, and driveways to get lost in. At some point in the future a connecting trail may be built between the southern terminus of the Upper Snoqualmie Trail and the Iron Horse State Park. For now, follow the paved road where you cross it, going south about 0.5

mile, and look for the Iron Horse State Park on your left. *Warning:* If the gate is closed, do not enter because the Water Department will have you arrested.

King County has plans to extend this trail to the west and connect it with the Snoqualmie Valley Trail. Combined, this would make a 40-mile trail between Duvall and Rattlesnake Lake.

31 Wallace Falls Railway Grade

Washington State Parks and Recreation Commission

Endpoints: Wallace Falls State Park parking lot to footbridge
Length: 2.3 miles
Surface: dirt and gravel
Restrictions: no horses
Original railroad: Wallace Lake Logging Company
Location: Gold Bar, Snohomish County
Latitude/longitude: N47° 51.83'/W121° 40.14'
Elevation: 268 feet at trailhead, 653 feet at footbridge

This is a delightful trail up an old logging railroad grade, which makes it steeper than most rail-trails. The canopy of trees is high, and there is always moisture in the lush underbrush and often on the trail. The trail is a well-worn route with many exposed rocks and is often wet or muddy. It is an alternative, parallel route to what is called the Woody Trail, which is open only to hikers and actually goes to Wallace Falls.

To reach Wallace Falls State Park, take Highway 2 to Gold Bar and turn left at the brown sign indicating the park. Follow signs for 2 more miles to the parking area.

This is a cool place to go on a hot day. The trail generally is canopied with trees. You can still see the large, old stumps of the first logging in this area. Now most of the trees are deciduous. The area gets a lot of rain, as evidenced by the abundance of moss and ferns. The park is very popular, so don't expect to be alone. The rail-trail is popular with mountain bicyclists, and a side rail-trail goes an additional 7 miles up to Wallace Lake.

The trail starts at the parking lot of Wallace Falls State Park at an elevation of 268 feet. It goes along a power line clear-cut area and

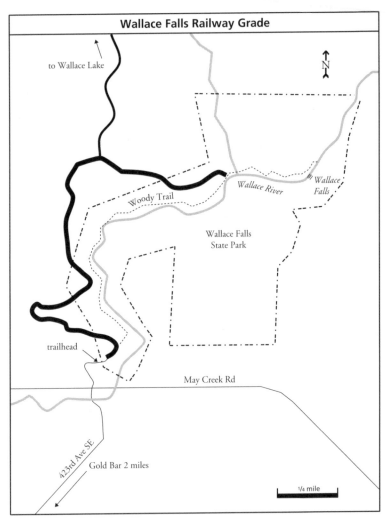

then enters the deep woods. At 0.4 mile the rail-trail continues to the left and the Woody Trail goes right. At 1.5 miles there is another railroad grade that turns left to Wallace Lake (unsigned), about 7 miles further. The rail-trail ends in 2.3 miles, and there is a short trail downhill that joins the Woody Trail.

Hikers can make a loop by hiking up the railway grade and down the Woody Trail. Hikers also can continue farther up the Woody Trail to the upper falls.

Children enjoying being outdoors

32 West Tiger Mountain Railroad Grade

Department of Natural Resources

Endpoints: Tiger Mountain Trail to Poo Poo Point Trail
Length: 4.0 miles
Surface: dirt
Restrictions: foot travel only
Original railroad: High Point Lumber Company
Location: Issaquah, King County
Latitude/longitude: N47° 31.20'/W121° 59.09'
Elevation: 1800 feet

Tiger Mountain State Park has numerous trails carved upward to Tiger Mountain's summits. This rail-trail is one of the few level trails on the mountain, although you must climb 1350 feet in elevation to get to it. The rail-trail lies on the grade of one of the numerous railroads that crisscrossed Tiger Mountain during the height of logging. This area originally was logged in the early part of the twentieth century, using railroads for access, before roads were common.

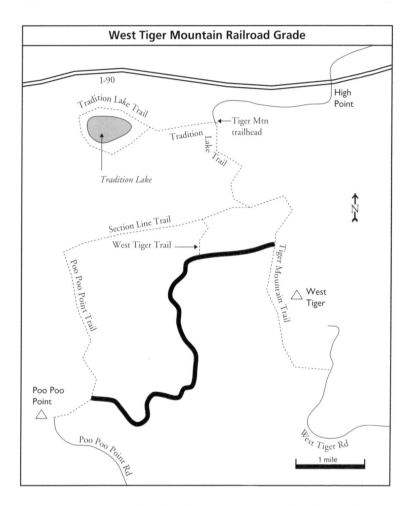

To get to the trailhead, take I-90 to exit 20 (High Point). Turn right and right again onto the frontage road and proceed to the Tiger Mountain State Forest parking area. Take the main trail uphill. Where the trees open up under a power line, take Tradition Lake Trail to the left. Stay on this trail as it climbs, with one trail going left and a second (Section Line Trail) going right. The trail gets steeper and crosses the railroad grade at about an elevation of 1800 feet. The trail right (west) contours around the mountain about 3 miles to the west side road. The trail going left (east) is quite well used to where it intersects Tiger Mountain Trail. To the east of this point the railroad grade is less worn and finally disappears into a creek bed in about 0.5 mile.

Several loops are possible with this rail-trail. You can make loops using the Section Line Trail, Poo Poo Point Trail, Tiger Mountain Trail, and Tradition Lake Trail. The Department of Natural Resources provides good up-to-date maps at the High Point parking area.

Although this area was completely logged until 1999, it is still

An old stump with the springboard cut still visible

a wonderful forest. The huge stumps of the original trees are still visible, with springboard cuts in their sides. Many of the trees that have grown since the logging era are now large deciduous trees. This means that they carpet the woods and trail with multicolored leaves in the fall and allow great views to the northwest in the winter. In the summer they provide welcome shade on hot days. Their canopy of green prevents significant brush from growing, allowing visitors to see long distances within the forest. They also help keep moisture from evaporating, so there is moss in many places.

part III

SOUTHWEST
WASHINGTON

33 Chehalis Western Trail

Thurston County Parks and Recreation

Endpoints: Lacey to 103rd Avenue Southeast
Length: 5.3 miles
Surface: asphalt
Restrictions: none
Original railroad: Chehalis Western Railroad, built 1926, abandoned 1986, trail opened 2000
Location: Lacey, Thurston County
Latitude/longitude: N47° 2.47'/W122° 50.71'
Elevation: 207 feet at Pacific Avenue, 254 feet at 103rd Avenue Southeast

This trail takes you from the busy Lacey business district out into the rolling hills and open grasslands to the south. It is named after the original railroad, the Chehalis Western Railroad, built by the Weyerhaeuser Company to get its logs down to Puget Sound.

To get to the north end, from I-5 take the Sleater Kinney Road Southeast exit and go south. Turn west on Pacific Avenue Southeast 0.25 mile and turn south at the "Leaving Lacey" sign in the middle of the street. Follow the overhead power lines behind Pacific Avenue businesses south and carefully cross the railroad tracks. The paved trail starts on the south side of the tracks. To get to the current south end, from I-5 take the Sleater Kinney Road Southeast exit and go south. Turn east on Pacific Avenue Southeast and south on College Street Southeast. Continue south on College Street Southeast, which when it turns becomes Rainier Road Southeast. Turn right (west) on Stedman Road Southeast for a mile and then right (west) onto 103rd Avenue Southeast.

The best starting point is the trailhead at 14th Avenue Southeast. From Sleater Kinney Road Southeast continue south past Pacific Avenue and turn right (west) onto 14th Avenue Southeast. Immediately after passing under the trail on the old railroad bridge turn left (south) to the trailhead. Here is a boat launch for Chambers Lake, restrooms, parking, and a good trail sign.

The first attraction south of the 14th Avenue Southeast trailhead is Chambers Lake, a long lake with abundant bird life. The trail then crosses 37th Avenue Southeast and heads into a wooded area east of Smith Lake. There is a new bridge over the Yelm Highway Southeast and a trailhead and access on the southwest side of this crossing.

The trail heads across more grassland, enters woods, and then does a tight left turn at the base of the Burlington Northern Santa Fe

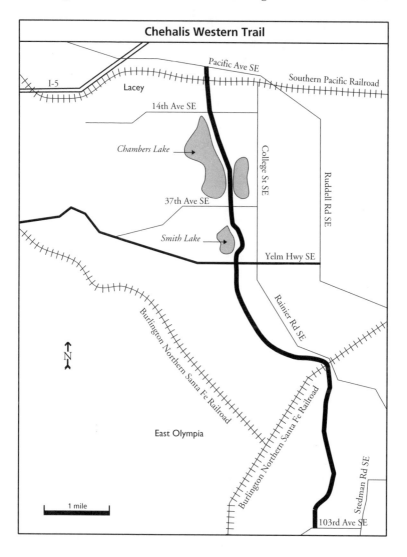

The wide paved and marked path

(BNSF) main-line tracks. The predecessor to BNSF had to build over the Chehalis Western Railroad tracks at this point, but when the Chehalis Western was abandoned, BNSF filled in the tunnel, so a detour is needed until the tunnel can be reopened for the trail. Follow the new trail north to Rainier Road Southeast. Turn right (east) a short distance and take the first small gravel road uphill to regain the trail.

From here south the trail is in the woods, although the trees have been cut back on both sides. Currently the trail ends at 103th Street Southeast, but Thurston County plans to continue the trail to the small logging community of Vail in the future, creating about a 25-mile-long trail into the mountains. It will also cross the Yelm to Tenino Trail, which is currently being planned.

34 Raymond—South Bend Trail

City of Raymond

Endpoints: Raymond to South Bend
Length: 4.0 miles
Surface: asphalt
Restrictions: none
Location: Raymond and South Bend, Grays Harbor County
Latitude/longitude: N46° 40.50'/W123° 42.22'
Elevation: 22 feet

This urban trail is part of the Willapa Hills Trail, operated by the Washington State Parks and Recreation Commission. This section was built and is maintained by the City of Raymond and the City of South Bend. It connects the communities of Raymond and South Bend with a nonmotorized route off the main highway.

To get to the east end, take SR 6 to Raymond, turn right onto US 101, and take the first left on Heath Street. Keep left and park in the parking area beyond the museum. The trail begins here and heads west. To get to the west end, take US 101 to South Bend and

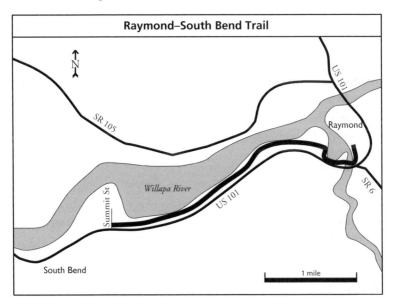

Raymond–South Bend Trail

The Chehalis River widens near the west end of the trail.

turn right on Summit Street before entering the business district of South Bend.

The trail starts in Raymond and goes over the Willapa River on the US 101 Bridge. The railroad went across its own swing bridge over the south fork of the Willapa River, but the bridge has not been rebuilt for nonmotorized use. The trail winds through the built-up shopping area before getting to the north side of US 101 and parallel to the Willapa River. There are good views of the Willapa River and benches to sit on and watch the birds and boats go by. The trail ends in downtown South Bend at a logging company loading yard.

Washington State Parks and Recreation Commission has plans to build the Willapa Hills Trail, which would go from the east end of this trail to Chehalis, and be part of the Washington Cross-State Trail.

35 Sylvia Creek Forestry Trail

Washington State Parks and Recreation Commission

Endpoint: Sylvia Lake
Length: 2.3 miles
Surface: dirt and gravel
Restrictions: none
Location: Montesano, Grays Harbor County
Latitude/longitude: N46° 59.82'/W123° 35.66'
Elevation: 127 feet

Two rail-trails, old and new, provide a wonderful opportunity to see beautiful Sylvia Lake, Sylvia Creek, and the surrounding forest. The old route follows the railroad grade along the edge of the lake. A new extension has been carved through the woods downstream along Sylvia Creek to show visitors the activities in a working forest.

To get to the trailhead, turn off SR 12 at Montesano and go north to the first stoplight. Turn left and then right onto Third Avenue. Go uphill and continue straight 1.5 miles to Sylvia Lake State Park. Turn left, cross the bridge over the lake, and park in the parking area on the left. Two rail-trails start from this point. The older trail goes east and north along the lake and is called the 2-Mile Trail. The newer trail starts next to the dam and heads downstream.

Sylvia Lake State Park is located on a beautiful lake created by a log dam in the early days of logging in the area. The land for the park was donated by the City of Montesano to the Washington State

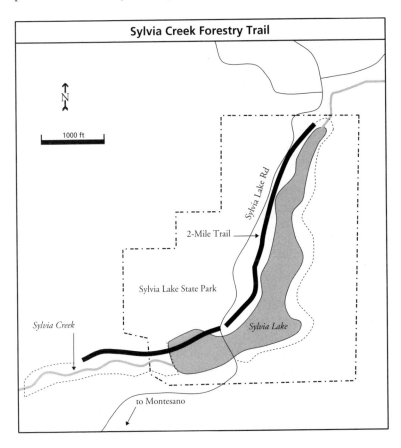

Sylvia Creek Forestry Trail

N

1000 ft

Sylvia Lake Rd

2-Mile Trail

Sylvia Lake State Park

Sylvia Creek

Sylvia Lake

to Montesano

Walking across the trestle over the log pond

Parks and Recreation Commission in 1936, and the park continues to be very popular, with a swimming area, camping, and trails.

The highlight of the trail is a bridge built in the lake behind the dam, which is barely above the water. This makes a unique boardwalk on water design that will never be repeated. The new trail is a project of the City of Montesano with the assistance of the Department of Natural Resources. There are plans to extend this trail down to Simpson Street in Montesano.

36 Woodard Bay Trail

Thurston County Parks and Recreation

Endpoints: Martin Way East to Woodard Bay
Length: 5.3 miles
Surface: asphalt
Restrictions: none
Original railroad: Chehalis Western Railway, built 1926, abandoned 1986, trail open 1998
Location: Lacey, Thurston County
Latitude/longitude: N47° 2.85'/W122° 50.42'
Elevation: 203 feet at Martin Way East, 36 feet at Woodard Bay

The Woodard Bay Trail begins in busy Lacey and transports you to the lush woods around Woodard Bay. It is a quiet, safe place for trail users in a rural area that is quickly becoming urbanized. The trail passes through mixed forest and open grassland.

To get to the south end, from I-5 take exit 109 (Sleater Kinney Road) and go west 0.9 mile to Martin Way East. The trailhead is a small gravel parking lot with a small sign on the north side of the road. Look for tall trees up on the railroad grade high above the road. To get to the north end trailhead at Woodard Bay, from I-5 take exit 109 west 0.6 mile to Sleater Kinney Road and take it north for 5 miles. Turn left on 56th Avenue Northeast, right on Shincke Road Northeast, and left on Woodard Bay Road. There is a Department of

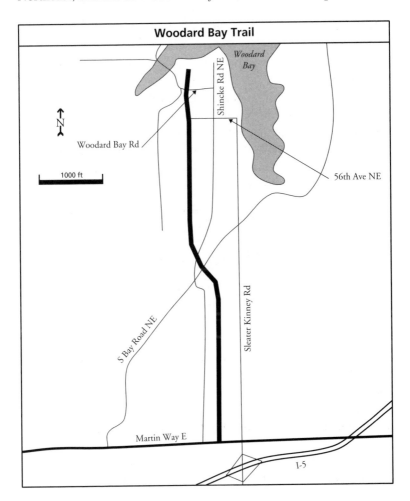

Woodard Bay Trail

Heading north into the heavy forest near Woodard Bay

Natural Resources trailhead on the right as you drop down to the bay.

The preferred starting point is the south end on Martin Way East, leading to a peaceful and quiet destination rather than a five-lane highway. The trail begins at Martin Way East and passes by the backyards of many homes, most hidden behind trees. Because the right-of-way is about 100 feet wide, hikers feel separated from these properties. Many of these adjacent landowners have built gates in their fences so that they might better access the trail.

In about 2.5 miles the trail crosses under South Bay Road Northeast and continues north along open grassy areas. It passes a small lake and then drops under the Woodard Bay Road. The Department of Natural Resources, which built the trail, did not want trail users to continue on to Woodard Bay because of their concern for adverse effects on the wildlife. So the department has blocked the railroad grade at this point, and the trail user must follow a narrow, winding hiking trail down to the Department of Natural Resources parking lot. This trailhead has ample parking, restrooms, and a ramp that enables people with disabilities to mount horses. There is a nature trail into the woods, but it is closed to all but foot traffic.

Thurston County Parks and Recreation would like to connect this trail with the Chehalis Western Trail on the south side of I-5. Unfortunately, when I-5 was built and Martin Way East was expanded, they removed both of the bridges, so it will be costly and difficult to get across these two obstacles. You can still find remnants of the filled grade if you look carefully going south.

part IV

EASTERN WASHINGTON

37 Ben Burr Trail

City of Spokane Parks

Endpoints: Liberty Park to Underhill Park
Length: 1.1 miles
Surface: dirt and gravel
Restrictions: none
Original railroad: Spokane and Inland Empire Electric Railroad, built 1905–1908, abandoned 1952–1970s, trail opened 1988
Location: Spokane, Spokane County
Latitude/longitude: N47° 37.10'/W117° 23.25'
Elevation: 1980 feet

This rail-trail is located in the southeast part of Spokane and connects two popular city parks, with good access at both ends. It is an ideal place for a quiet walk or for jogging. Because the trail is elevated above neighboring houses, there are good views of Spokane and Mount Spokane to the north.

The Spokane and Inland Empire Electric Railroad originally was built to move passengers and freight in the fast-growing Palouse farmland. It extended south to Colfax and Moscow, Idaho, and east to Coeur d'Alene. Passenger service ended on March 31, 1939, and

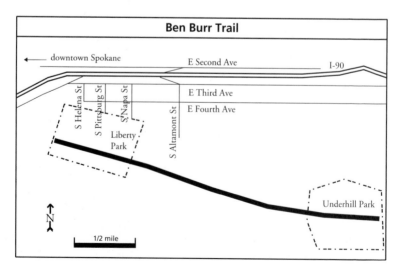

the last freight service ended in October 1941. Portions of the line were abandoned in 1952, with the last sections of line removed in the late 1970s. The trail is named after Ben Burr, a former chief civil engineer for the Great Northern Railroad.

To get to the west end, take I-90 to Spokane and exit 283A (Altamont). Turn right on Altamont and go one block to East 4th Avenue. Follow East 4th Avenue back to the west and turn left into Liberty Park at the park sign facing the freeway. The rail-trail begins at the south end of the parking area.

The trail is still in its rustic state from years of neglect. There have been few improvements along the route except for a bridge over Altamont and a concrete ramp up from Liberty Park. The remainder of the trail is in a rough, natural state with a rocky surface and brush growing alongside. This preserves its ambience as an old natural corridor in the midst of an urban area.

The trail connects two community parks, Underhill and Liberty. These parks have parking, restrooms, and ball fields. At the west end of the trail is a large brick building sitting high on the hill. This was the main power-generating facility for the electric line and has been converted into apartments.

The rail-trail is a community development project of the South Central Community. Sometime in the future it may connect with the old railroad route going south from South Hill, near Glenrose, to Colfax, and connect to the north to the Spokane River Centennial Trail.

Looking down from the rocky cliffs along the trail

38 Bill Chippman Palouse Pathway

Pullman Parks and Recreation, Moscow Parks and Recreation

Endpoints: Pullman, Washington, and Moscow, Idaho
Length: 6.3 miles
Surface: paved
Restrictions: no horses
Location: Pullman, Washington; and Moscow, Idaho
Latitude/longitude: N46° 43.29'/W117° 9.85'
Elevation: 2379 feet at Pullman, 2543 feet at Moscow

This pathway is a great nonmotorized route between two college towns and a great place to take kids for walks, bicycling, or in-line skating. It is almost flat and is wide enough for all users to share and enjoy. It is an unusual public amenity in an area of very hilly land where most valleys are plugged with roads.

To get to the east end in Moscow, take SR 270 into Moscow, turn north at Perimeter Road, and park in the Palouse Mall shopping center parking lot. Cross back over SR 270 and turn west onto the path. All the property to the south of SR 270 is part of the University of Idaho and is closed to public parking. To get to the west end, take SR 270 into Pullman and turn south on Bishop Boulevard, the first light going into town from the east. Turn left in about two blocks into a small parking area. The trail begins at Bishop Boulevard.

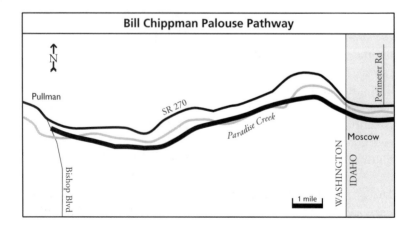

Children enjoying a safe ride

The trail parallels the main four-lane highway the entire distance. Although you always hear the highway noise, the trail wanders back and forth in terms of distance from the road, providing some relief. It crosses Paradise Creek numerous times, providing an opportunity to watch the birds and other forms of wildlife that thrive near the water. There are portable toilets and emergency phones at milepost (MP) 1.5 and MP 5.0 (measured from Pullman). The trail continues going east through a portion of the University of Idaho campus but does not go into downtown Moscow.

There are plans for both Pullman and Moscow to build loop trails in each city that connect to this trail.

39 Coal Mines Trail

Coal Mines Trail Commission

Endpoints: Cle Elum to Ronald
Length: 2.3 miles
Surface: gravel and ballast
Restrictions: none; open to snowmobiles
Location: Cle Elum and Roslyn, Kittitas County
Latitude/longitude: N47° 11.83'/W120° 56.69'
Elevation: 1926 feet at Cle Elum, 2382 feet at Ronald

This trail follows the route of a rail line built specifically for hauling coal from the numerous mines that were built in this valley.

There are interpretive signs along the entire trail, number coded to a history pamphlet available at the Chamber of Commerce building located just south of the trailhead.

To get to the south trailhead, take exit 83 from I-90 and go through Cle Elum. Turn north at Stafford Road across from the sign to South Cle Elum and the Chamber of Commerce information building. Go one block north to the trailhead. To get to the north end, take SR 903 north through Roslyn to the general store in Ronald. Take the first gravel road north of the general store and meet the trail in 100 yards.

The trail begins in Cle Elum and climbs at a moderate grade up to Ronald. It follows Crystal Creek north and is hidden from neighboring homes and roads for most of the way except where it passes through Roslyn. There are a few territorial views from the trail, but most of the time the thick trees hide the adjacent land.

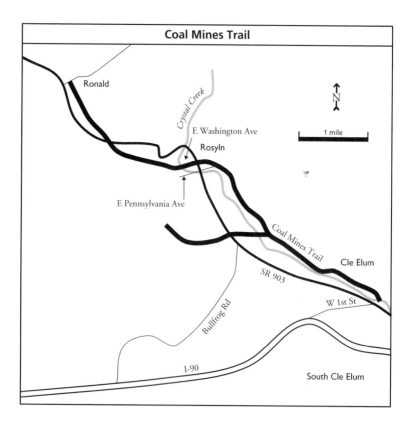

The famous Roslyn Café

At about 0.5 mile is a Y where a branch line went west to the Number 9 mine, closed in 1963. The trail skirts the east edge of Roslyn and then turns west and passes through three blocks of the main part of Roslyn following East Washington Avenue. Roslyn used to be a rough-and-tumble coal mine town, but today it is best known as the place where *Northern Exposure* was filmed. To find the Roslyn Cafe, featured in the TV show, go two blocks south to East Pennsylvania Avenue. There is also a general store that rents and repairs bikes at the corner of East Pennsylvania Avenue and SR 903.

Leaving Roslyn going northwest, the trail passes by Runje Field, a large park and playfield complex with restrooms, picnic tables, and water. The trail north of here is bordered by thin trees with few views as the trail climbs higher. It crosses SR 903 and then in 0.5 mile ends in Ronald at the wire fence. Take the gravel road just before the fence and go downhill a short distance to the Ronald General Store.

It is recommended that you start at Cle Elum on this trail so that you will have an easier trip coming back. This trail is open to snowmobiles in the winter, and because it is so narrow it probably is not suitable for snowshoes or cross-country skiing.

40 Columbia Plateau Trail

Washington State Parks and Recreation Commission

Endpoints: Fish Lake to East Pasco
Length: 132.0 miles
Surface: asphalt, gravel, rough ballast
Restrictions: 24 miles improved
Original railroad: Spokane, Portland, and Seattle Railroad, built 1908, abandoned 1991
Location: Cheney, Spokane County, to Pasco, Franklin County
Latitude/longitude: N47° 31.35'/W117° 30.95'
Elevation: 2200 feet at Fish Lake, 2062 feet at Martin Road.

This railroad corridor has several special attributes. The right-of-way on both sides of the grade is a natural area, and the corridor is surrounded by land that is almost completely undeveloped. There is extensive railroad history, part of which is preserved in the railroad grade itself. The route was one of the state's early transportation corridors. It also follows the path of a major geologic event that had a significant impact on eastern Washington.

Between 12,000 and 14,000 years ago a series of tremendous floods caused by broken ice dams in Montana roared through most of southeastern Washington. The Bretz Floods, named after the geologist who identified their existence, covered Spokane in more than 800 feet of water. The tremendous volume of water flowed south down to the Columbia River, scouring gullies in the solid basalt rock from the Palouse Hills west to the Cascades. The resulting land has been called the scablands because the land is still trying to heal itself from the flood's scouring of the topsoil. The rail-trail follows the path of the floodwaters, whose power is still visible along the entire route.

The Spokane, Portland, and Seattle Railroad built this line. Although it was not the first rail line connecting Spokane southwest to Portland, it was designed to be the best, with the easiest grades and gentlest curves. Much of the railroad right-of-way follows the route of the Mullen Trail. This 644-mile wagon route was established in 1868 but abandoned in 1872, when railroads began to provide faster transportation. There are several markers of this route along the corridor. The Washington Historical Society erected a stone monument in Lamont in 1925, showing where the Mullen Trail passed.

The dry weather is kind to artifacts. You can still see old buildings

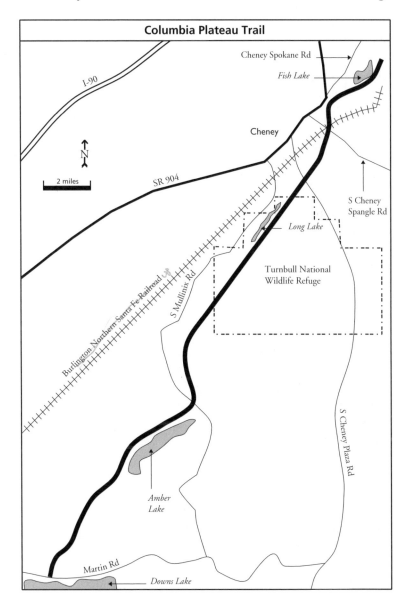

Columbia Plateau Trail

Cheney Spokane Rd

Fish Lake

I-90

N

2 miles

SR 904

Cheney

S Cheney Spangle Rd

Long Lake

Turnbull National Wildlife Refuge

Burlington Northern Santa Fe Railroad

S Mullinix Rd

S Cheney Plaza Rd

Amber Lake

Martin Rd

Downs Lake

that were built at the turn of the century. The grain elevators built along the railroad also attest to the importance of the railroad to the area's growth. The old water tower at Benge is still in good condition and is used as the town's water storage facility.

This corridor generally is undeveloped except for some grazing areas and a few farms. It provides a wonderful opportunity for viewing wildlife. There are numerous rock depressions, caused by the great floods, which hold water year-round, providing invaluable habitat for wildlife in an otherwise very dry part of the state.

The construction of the railroad itself actually created wildlife habitat. In many places the gravel grade has created small ponds that have become nesting sites for birds. Numerous cuts in the rock along this route have become natural home sites for owls, rattlesnakes, and other animals. The lower part of the corridor alongside the Snake River passes through ideal habitat for large raptors. The four steel trestles provide airy nesting sites for swallows.

To get to the north end of the trail, take I-90 to Cheney. Go 3 miles northeast on Spokane–Cheney Road to Myers Park Road at the north end of Fish Lake. This is a county park with parking, toilets, water access to Fish Lake, and a food concession (in season). There is a state park trailhead area at MP 365. The trail goes south from here and is paved asphalt for 3.75 miles. It is a steady, gradual climb to the end of the asphalt at the Cheney Trailhead (MP 361.25) off the Cheney Spangle Road. There are large ditches on both sides of the trail that sometimes are filled with rushing water. Most of the trail is cut through the rock, which can provide shade but also reflect and hold the sun's heat on hot days.

At the Cheney trailhead there are restrooms, shaded picnic benches, and good parking for horse trailers. The trail heads straight south from here and is unpaved. The surface is a hard-packed gravel that is ideal for walking, bicycling, and horseback riding, and even for strong wheelchair users. For the first mile, the trail passes through an open, flat, grassy area with private property on both sides. It passes under the S Cheney Plaza Road and enters the Turnbull National Wildlife Refuge at MP 360. Here are small ponds and lakes with sparse pine trees, creating a rich wildlife habitat. Ducks Unlimited, a private nonprofit group, also owns some property adjacent to the corridor that is being preserved for the same purpose. The trail user can view these special areas because the corridor often passes close to ponds, lakes, and creeks. This is to be expected because the railroad's engineers sought out waterways, which are naturally gradual paths through rocky landscapes. Some of the landowners adjacent to the corridor have also set aside their lands as wildlife preserves. Please stay on the trail to help preserve this natural setting.

At MP 358 there is a large lake to the west, Long Lake. There is a toilet 4.75 miles south of the Cheney Trailhead. The trail passes through the Turnbull National Wildlife Refuge for 4 miles. The trail from Cheney trailhead has been straight until milepost MP 354, where there is a slight turn to the east and a deep cut in the rocks. Watch for owls perching on the rocks in these deep cuts. This point is the high point for this line going from Spokane to Pasco. It is all downhill from here. At MP 349 is Amber Lake, with public lake access, trailhead parking, and toilets.

As you continue south, the pine trees disappear and the reward is extensive vistas. To the south and east you can view the western edge of the Palouse, an area where topsoil was created from volcanoes along the Cascades, creating very good soil for growing wheat and other crops. The tradeoff for great views is that there is no shelter from the wind or sun, so be prepared. The next trailhead is at Martin Road at MP 341, with parking, toilets, and a picnic area. Be sure to look at the railroad grade going south. The engineers had to build a fill across the coulee by moving gravel from the hillside and filling across the valley. This fill is more than 1 mile long, and the scars from where the fill material was gathered are still very clear around the north end. The segment going south to Lamont is not scheduled for completion for years.

The trail south of Martin Road (not illustrated on the map) has not been improved and consists of heavy rock ballast, making travel very difficult. Sections of the trail will be improved over time, starting from the Snake River end. South of Martin Road, the grade enters a region of more rugged rock cliffs and small lakes on its way to Lamont. Lamont boasts a new school, a few houses, and a grain elevator located alongside the old railroad grade. There are no public facilities in Lamont.

South of Lamont the corridor follows several dry washes for 23

The gravel trail stretches to the horizon south of Cheney.

miles to Benge. This is one of the most remote stretches of the entire route, with no roads alongside or crossing it for miles. The highlight is where the trail crosses over the Milwaukee Road Corridor trail, out in the middle of the scablands. Benge is a very small town with a grocery that at one time was open daily from 8:00 A.M. to 5:00 P.M. except Sundays and holidays. There is a small town park across the street from the grocery.

South of Benge the grade enters Cow Creek, which goes north to Sprague and is one of the largest drainages in the region. Between Benge and Kahlotus the canyons get larger and the cliffs steeper. Near Ankeny the grade passes across a large steel trestle and then over the Union Pacific's active line just before that line enters a tunnel, a very scenic place to watch trains. Below are the lush green pastures fed by the water from Cow Creek. Across the valley next to the road is a historical marker describing the Mullen Trail. In the valley below you can see a stone house, one of several built by early settlers who were attracted to Cow Creek because of the water it supplied.

At Hooper Junction the railroad parallels SR 26, the site of another Mullen Trail historic sign. The grade passes under the highway and across a second large steel trestle to Washtucna, named after a local Indian chief. The railroad surveyors were so intent on keeping an easy grade that it ended up part-way up the ridge 0.25 mile southeast of town. Farther south the corridor is located across the valley between Washtucna and Kahlotus and skirts the south side of Lake Kahlotus. *Kahlotus* is an Indian name meaning "hole in the ground," which describes the feeling you have being on the valley floor of the Washtucna Coulee.

At Kahlotus the grade enters a tunnel into Devil's Canyon, a steep, narrow canyon dropping quickly to the Snake River. The railroad could not match the steep grade of the canyon and therefore was carved along the rocky hillside. Rounding the corner that overlooks the Snake River through another tunnel, you will be greeted with a spectacular view of the lower Snake River Canyon. Below is the old railroad grade; the portions downstream were flooded when the Ice Harbor Dam was built. Heading downstream, pass over four tall steel trestles over Box, Wilson, Bouvey, and Burr Canyons. These steel structures were built in 1908 by the American Bridge Company and are listed on the state and federal historical registers.

As you pass along this route you can hear the rumble of the trains from the south side of the Snake River and watch boats far below. Numerous birds live on the rocky cliffs next to the grade and in the trestle girders. There are some public facilities, including campgrounds and restrooms, at Lower Monumental Dam and Ice Harbor Dam.

The grade gradually descends closer to the Snake River by the time it reaches Pasco. The current trail ends where it crosses Mehlenbacker Farm Road. There is good access to the river via this road.

To get to the south end, take SR 12 through Pasco to Pasco–Kahlotus Road and proceed east 4.8 miles. Turn right (south) on Martindale Road, signed "Dead End" and "Primitive Road." Go 1.4 miles and angle left on Mehlenbacker Farm Road for 0.8 mile to the grade. The Washington State Parks and Recreation Commission plans to develop the trail from Ice Harbor Trailhead (MP 241.5) to Snake River Junction (MP 256.5) in 2001. There is good access to the Snake River here. Sacajawea State Park is across SR 12 in the opposite direction at the confluence of the Columbia and Snake Rivers. Other good access point are at Lamont, Benge, Washtucna, and Kahlotus.

Be well prepared when you travel this rail-trail. The only dependable drinking water is found at Fish Lake, Lamont, Benge, Washtucna, and Kahlotus. Washtucna has a grocery store, restaurants, and a motel. Kahlotus has a restaurant. Carry food, water, maps, and a snakebite kit. Roads crossing the corridor are few and far between. The best time to travel this corridor is from April through June and in the fall.

41 Cowiche Canyon Trail

Cowiche Canyon Conservancy

Endpoints: Weikel Road to trail end
Length: 3.0 miles
Surface: natural dirt and gravel
Restrictions: no hunting, no firearms
Original railroad: North Yakima and Valley Railroad
Location: 11 miles west of Yakima, Yakima County
Latitude/longitude: N46° 42.32'/W120° 45.12'
Elevation: 1915 feet

A unique oasis in the dry sagebrush of eastern Washington, Cowiche Canyon is a beautiful, pristine canyon. The rail-trail follows an abandoned railroad grade through a narrow canyon cut into the rock by Cowiche Creek and provides visitors a quiet place of rock, wildlife, and vegetation. To get to the trailhead, take I-82 to exit 33 (Yakima) and turn west onto East Yakima Avenue. Go 1.8 miles west and turn right on Summitview. Go 9.7 miles and turn right on Weikel Road. Go 0.4 mile to the Cowiche Canyon Trail sign on the right. Turn

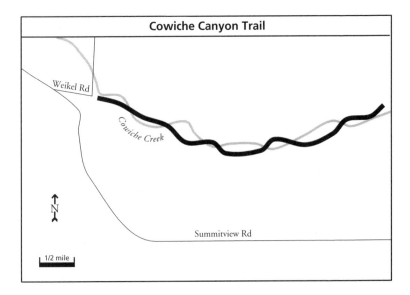

Cowiche Canyon Trail

Weikel Rd

Cowiche Creek

N

Summitview Rd

1/2 mile

right and park in the large, open gravel area.

This trail is ideal for walking. The narrow canyon has a quiet peacefulness, with the creek underfoot and wildlife everywhere. Although bicyclists can use the trail, it is not a long ride and probably will remain a dead end for many years to come.

The trail starts at the east end of the canyon with a large wooden sign describing the canyon and illustrating the trail and creek. It winds down the canyon, crossing and recrossing the creek for 1.7 miles to a missing bridge. Although the creek is not very wide, even in late summer there is still water, enough that you will get wet wading across it. The trail continues another 1.3 miles before ending at private property.

The canyon is a haven for naturalists, with numerous

An aerial view of the green swath cut by the Cowiche Canyon

birds and small animals thriving in the grasses nurtured by the flowing creek. The area is free of development and is close to its natural state. The green swath along the creek is in strong contrast to the neighboring sagebrush and rock.

The north and south walls of the canyon differ because the south wall is 13 million years older than the north wall. Fourteen million years ago, lava flowed from fissures near Pullman to form the flora and south wall. One million years ago, Tieton andesite from the Goat Rocks Range created the north wall. As the trail runs back and forth across the creek, it cuts through parts of the south and north walls close enough for the visitor to see the differences in rock type.

This trail is owned and operated by the Cowiche Canyon Conservancy, a private nonprofit group that is preserving a unique ecosystem with public access. One of the main goals of the conservancy is to preserve the land in as much of its natural state as possible.

42 Douglas Creek Trail

Bureau of Land Management

Endpoints: Palisades to Alstown
Length: 10.0 miles
Surface: original ballast, sand, and rock
Restrictions: none
Location: 3 miles southeast of Waterville, Douglas County
Latitude/longitude: N47° 27.23'/W119° 52.66'
Elevation: 1099 feet at bottom, 2160 feet at Alstown

This rail-trail is located in a little-known part of the state with a unique natural beauty. The trail connects the low, dry sagebrush of Moses Coulee with the high plateau farmlands near Waterville. If you are tired of crowded trails, this is a place to find solitude.

The land just east of the Columbia River is normally very arid, especially at lower elevations. The existence of water has a significant effect on the vegetation and wildlife. Badger Mountain to the west of Douglas Creek provides a continuous water supply to Douglas Creek, even in the heat of summer. McCue Spring, near the south end of the trail, provides additional water year-round.

To get to the south end of the trail, take SR 26 south of Wenatchee 15 miles to Palisades Road SW. Go east 12 miles up Moses Coulee past Palisades to where the road turns sharply to the right. Take the first good gravel road left (north) up the hill to the left of Douglas Creek Canyon. Proceed into the canyon before parking. To get to the north end of the trail, take SR 2 to Waterville, go 1 mile east, and take Road K SW southeast 3 miles to Alstown, where there is a silver-colored grain terminal.

This is a newly acquired rail-trail, and development has just begun. The condition of the trail reflects the harshness of the surroundings. The surface varies from large rocks to sand. There are numerous gravel berms where the original culverts were removed. The missing trestles necessitate fording the creek, but in the summer the cool water is a delight. The trail is difficult for mountain biking; hiking and horseback riding are much more appropriate.

Before you visit this rail-trail, contact the Bureau of Land Management in Wenatchee to learn the latest conditions. Also, be prepared for a very rustic hike in a remote area. Pack plenty of water and provisions and be especially careful of rattlesnakes—they love

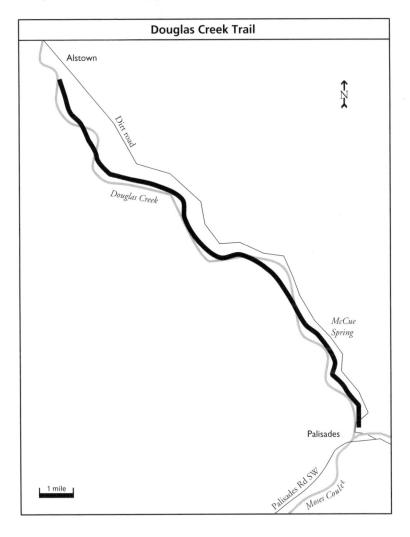

The rugged country carved out by Douglas Creek

the rocky canyon walls. One of the greatest assets of this location is that you are not likely to see anyone along the trail, but it can also be the greatest danger.

43 Iron Horse State Park

Washington State Parks and Recreation Commission

Endpoints: Rattlesnake Lake to Columbia River
Length: 100.0 miles
Surface: unimproved ballast and dirt
Restrictions: no hunting, camping in designated areas only
Original railroad: Chicago, Milwaukee, St. Paul, and Pacific Railroad
Location: Cedar Falls, King County; Hyak, Ellensburg, and Kittitas, Kittitas County
Latitude/longitude: N47° 25.86'/W121° 45.99'
Elevation: 998 feet at Rattlesnake Lake, 2562 feet at Hyak, 510 feet at Columbia River Bridge

The Iron Horse State Park is a spectacular example of a rural rail-trail. It takes the traveler from the edges of the Seattle area suburbs to the dry steppe shrub and beauty of the Columbia River. It includes the longest tunnel for nonmotorized use on any trail in the United States, the 2.25-mile-long Snoqualmie Tunnel. It has numerous bridges, tunnels, and viewpoints all along its 100-mile route.

To get to the western trailhead, take I-90 to exit 32 (436th Avenue Southeast). Turn right on Cedar Falls Road Southeast and proceed 3.5 miles to Rattlesnake Lake. There is a large gravel parking area on your right. Please note that cars are towed if left in this parking area after dark. To get to the trail, continue on the asphalt road another 0.25 mile and look for the railroad grade on your left. The Upper Snoqualmie Valley Trail leaves the parking area and goes downhill back to North Bend. To get to the east end of Iron Horse State Park, from I-90 at Vantage, take Huntzinger Road south past the Wanapum Dam until you see the railroad bridge to the east. The trail begins at the railroad crossing of Huntzinger Road.

Unlike many lowland rail-trails, this rail-trail goes up and down to make it over the mountains. It begins at 998 feet near Rattlesnake Lake, climbs to 2562 feet at the east portal of the Snoqualmie Tunnel, down to 1590 feet in Ellensburg, back up to 2550 feet at the east portal of the Boylston Tunnel, and down to 510 feet at the west end of the Columbia River Bridge.

There are many access points along this 100-mile-long trail, including the following:

▌ **Twin Falls parking lot:** From I-90 take exit 34. Turn right and take the first right into the Twin Falls State Park parking lot. Follow the road uphill to the grade.

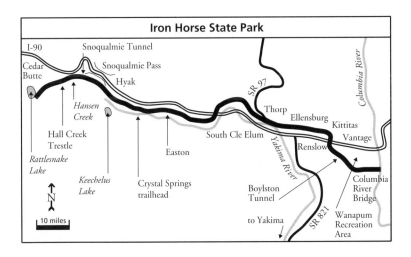

▮ **McClellan Butte:** From I-90 take exit 38 and follow directions to the McClellan Butte trailhead. In about 1 mile this trail crosses the Iron Horse Trail at mile 13.1 and continues up to the top of McClellan Butte another 3700 feet above

▮ **Hansen Creek Trestle:** There is access to this trestle from the Hansen Creek Forest Service Road 5510, off exit 45 from I-90. The access trail starts about 200 yards up the road from the trestle on the left (east) side. The first 50 feet are straight up, then it becomes easier. This access trail gains the railroad grade just beyond the east end of the trestle.

▮ **Annette Lake Trail:** From I-90 take exit 47. The Annette Lake trailhead parking is 0.5 mile downhill from this point.

▮ **Hyak Trailhead:** From I-90 take exit 54 (Hyak). Go south and turn left onto the access road on the south side of the freeway. Go 0.125 mile and turn right on the first road, Forest Service Road 22191. Take an immediate right up the hill on an access road signed to the Hyak Trailhead.

▮ **Keechelus Lake Trailhead:** Take I-90 to exit 54 (Hyak). Take the first left along the frontage road and then the first right on Forest Service Road 22191 for 0.25 mile.

▮ **Crystal Springs:** From I-90 take exit 62 and go south about 1 mile. There is a large signed trailhead parking area on the right.

▮ **Easton:** From I-90 take exit 71, go straight at the stop sign and continue up the hill. Turn left just past the fire hall down a long gravel driveway to reach the trailhead on the right.

▮ **West Nelson Siding:** From I-90 take exit 74 (West Nelson Siding) and go south 200 yards.

▮ **Golf Course Road:** From I-90 take exit 78 (Golf Course Road) and go south 200 yards.

▮ **South Cle Elum Trailhead:** From I-90 take exit 84 and go west into Cle Elum. Turn south on Reed Street, marked with a sign to South Cle Elum (a separate city). Go south across the Yakima River, and Reed Street becomes East Fourth Street. Turn right on Madison and in two blocks left onto West 6th Street. Turn right onto Milwaukee Avenue, and the trailhead is on your left at West 7th Street. If you continue south across the trail on West 6th Street you will come to the Iron Horse Bed and Breakfast, located at the site of the old train crew housing. They also have two cabooses that are closer to the trail.

- ❚ **Thorp:** From I-90 take exit 93 and go north a short distance to where the trail crosses Thorp Road.
- ❚ **SR 97:** SR 97 crosses the trail about 3 miles west of Ellensburg.
- ❚ **Ellensburg:** From I-90 take exit 106 (Ellensburg) and go north. Turn right on Cascade Way and follow it as it makes a right turn, but remains Cascade Way. Follow Cascade Way into town and turn left on North Water Street, which crosses the grade in about 0.25 mile.
- ❚ **Kittitas:** From I-90 take exit 115 (Kittitas) and go north. The road crosses the trail.
- ❚ **Boylston Tunnel:** From I-90 take exit 115 (Kittitas). Go east on the Kittitas Highway to Mundy Road. Turn south over I-90 and take the first left. Take the first right just after you pass under the railroad trestle and follow it up to the tunnel.

The starting point for the western end of this trail is at Rattlesnake Lake, just south of North Bend. This is a great lake for swimming when it is open. King County has a trail, the Upper Snoqualmie Valley Trail, which goes northwest down to North Bend. King County also has plans to build a trail from the west end of Iron Horse State Park through the City of Seattle watershed to connect with the Cedar River Trail at Landsburg and the Enumclaw Plateau Trail at Bagley Junction. At some point in the future, the Washington State Parks and Recreation Commission may also have a separate trailhead.

The trail starts out as a narrow, tree-lined route that skirts around the base of Cedar Butte. Since the railroad stopped spraying, the deciduous trees have invaded the edges of the railroad bed and grown quite large in 20 years. Soon this will be a complete canopy of trees. Look for a small waterfall on your right that usually has water year-round.

As you start hearing the freeway noise grow louder, you will come to a power substation right in the middle of the trail. Puget Power got permission to use the right-of-way to transmit power generated by the Twin Falls hydroelectric project, which has hidden the turbines from public view. Just east of this substation is a road down to the Twin Falls State Park parking area, exit 34 from I-90.

Next you will pass some steep rock cliffs that are popular with rock climbers. Watch out for falling rock and ropes stretched across the trail. This is such a popular area for climbers that a book has been written just for the routes on this rock.

Past the rock climbing area, cross the rebuilt Hall Creek Trestle. The original trestle was destroyed by a flood caused by excessive logging on public lands upstream of the trestle, and was rebuilt in 1999. The trestles provide some of the best places for viewing because there are often trees or rock walls lining the trail elsewhere.

In about a mile the McClellan Butte Trail crosses the grade, climbing to an elevation of almost 5000 feet. Next, cross Hansen Creek, where you can see a forest road below. There is access to this road at the east end of the trestle via a trail that goes south, with a steep drop to the road at the end. Hansen Creek Trestle, located at mile 18.7, is another access point and a place with spectacular views. This trestle is easy to identify because it is a very long steel trestle on a curve with five overhead supports used to hold the electric lines that ran the train like an electric trolley. It is also covered with large, pink ballast rocks.

The Annette Lake Trail crosses the trail at the next trestle. It is a very popular hike and goes to a small, beautiful lake. Just east of the Annette Lake Trail crossing is an unusual trail structure: a wooden snow shed still in good condition. This snow shed was built to protect winter travelers from avalanches, but the Washington State Parks and Recreation Commission has closed it, so be very careful if you travel this route in the snow season.

Once you are east of the shed, look back above the shed and see the hilltop scoured of all large trees. The trail generally is well sheltered from avalanches for winter travel, but always check the weather reports.

Round the corner beyond to get even better views of the Cascade Mountain peaks near Snoqualmie Pass.

The highlight of this trail is the tunnel, partly because it is so unique, partly because it is so cool. It stays about 54 degrees Fahrenheit during the part of the year it is open (May through October). It is closed during the winter because the icicles that form on the roof of the tunnel might fall and hurt trail users. If you are traveling east you cannot see the light at the end of the tunnel because just 10 feet from the portal the grade turns south and the hill blocks most of the light. But looking back west, you can continue to see the light. The tunnel was built between 1912 and 1914 and at 2.25 miles is one of the longest on the entire line, stretching to Chicago, Illinois.

Tunnel just east of the Yakima River near Easton

The inside of the tunnel is flat, smooth gravel, with water drains on both sides. Tunnels are notorious for holding water, and this one has large gutters on both sides, covered with wood and gravel. It is very dark, so be sure to bring a flashlight. There are no lights in the tunnel, but there are reflectors on the sides of the walls.

At Hyak there is a huge parking lot and trailhead. This is a very popular place because people can easily walk into the tunnel from here in the summer, and it is a great starting point going east for cross-country skiing in the winter. The trail east of here hugs the south shore of Keechelus Lake, with great views across the lake. The access to the lake usually is down a steep embankment, but there are safe places to descend. There used to be two snow sheds along this route, but the Washington State Parks and Recreation Commission removed them. Be very cautious passing under the places where the snow sheds used to sit because they were built in avalanche-prone areas.

Soon after Lake Keechelus is the Crystal Springs Trailhead. This is a large trailhead with a campground and parking for horse trailers. There is access to I-90 if you head north. The road that crosses the trail goes up to Stampede Pass, the site of another railroad line, still active. The trees are thinner on this side of the mountains, there are more pines, and the trail stretches in front of you for several miles. If you listen carefully, you can hear the trains going by on the Stampede Pass rail line, which is just uphill.

Just after Cabin Creek Road crosses the trail, there is an open area where the BPA high-voltage transmission lines pass. They cut down all trees beneath the lines to prevent arcing across to the treetops. Just past the power lines the trail crosses over Yakima River on a rebuilt bridge. Here you have great views of Lake Easton. The trail also crosses the main-line BNSF Railway Stampede Pass line. It passes through a short tunnel and is high above the lake.

The trail comes out at a diversion dam that pulls water from Lake Easton for irrigation use downstream. Be very careful passing this canal because there are no guardrails and it is impossible to climb out of the canal. The trail then enters the backside of Easton and passes through to the Easton Trailhead, a gravel parking lot on the south side of the grade.

South Cle Elum is 11.4 miles from here. The trail parallels both I-90 and the Stampede Pass active rail line. Although you can hear the freeway at times, it is usually out of sight. Pass over a few bridges and then drift into South Cle Elum. South Cle Elum is a distinct city from Cle Elum, created by a competing railroad. The animosity still simmers. As you come into South Cle Elum you will see two large structures on the left. The tall brick building is the old power station, used to generate the power electricity for the railroad. The second building is the old railroad station, the last one still standing on this line in Washington State. The Washington State Parks and Recreation Commission owns both of these buildings and hopes to renovate them as a museum and trailhead building. Currently the trailhead is located just east on the north side of the trail. If you want to stay the night, accommodations are available at the Iron Horse Bed and Breakfast on the south side of the trail, built in the old Milwaukee Road crew house.

The next few miles of trail parallel and then duck under I-90. The trail heads into a narrow canyon leading to Thorp, 18.6 miles from South Cle Elum. This is one of the more scenic sections of the trail and one of the few that is distant from I-90. The trail winds through this narrow canyon close to the Yakima River. It passes through several short tunnels that make ideal places to rest in a cool spot out of the sun in the summer. This section usually is not covered with snow in the winter, but would make a great cross-country route if it were. Across the river on the north side are the main-line BNSF tracks that go west over Stampede Pass.

The trail comes out of the canyon and passes near the small community of Thorp, which in railroad days was much larger. Continuing east, cross the Yakima River a second time and then cross the BNSF line and SR 10. There is no good access from SR 10 because the rail line is elevated. To access the grade here, go east a short distance and take a shortcut road to SR 97, where the trail crosses at grade.

From Thorp it is 6.8 miles to Ellensburg. The railroad ran right through Ellensburg, and gradually Central Washington University grew up around the railroad. However, the university does not want public trail users, especially horseback riders, to go through its campus, so the trail has been blocked off with fences and buildings. But you can wind around these obstacles and still follow the original railroad grade by staying under the power lines as much as possible. There will be an official detour going north around campus in the future that probably will return to the grade at the county fairgrounds just east of the campus. The main business district of Ellensburg is about eight blocks south and eight blocks west of where the grade crosses through the university. It is sad that the largest community on the entire Washington Cross-State Trail is so opposed to the trail when it has very little impact on the majority of the town.

Going east from Ellensburg the trail begins a climb to the Boylston Tunnel. It is out in the open now, passing by farms and soon passing through the small community of Kittitas. There is a nice little park to the south of the grade where it crosses the main street through town. This is the last of civilization you'll see all the way to the Columbia River, so stock up. It is a very small community, with the old train station preserved as a museum, public meeting place, and park area. This is the last chance for potable water until Wanapum Recreation Area on the Columbia River. This is very dry country, and all users should be prepared with adequate water and food. There are no services on the trail east of here, and generally there are no public roads nearby.

About 3 miles east of Kittitas, at a place called Renslow, the railroad crosses I-90 on a long trestle that is blocked temporarily. To cross the freeway, about 2 miles east of Kittitas take the freeway crossing just south of the grade and turn left (east) on the frontage Boylston Road on the south side of the freeway. Pass under the trestle and take the first road to the right, Boylston Road, which leads back up to the grade. You can find the grade by looking for the power lines. You can also scramble up the grade at the trestle approaches if you are careful.

Boylston is located at the west end of the Boylston Tunnel. At one time there were several sidings here to store trains and helper engines to get up the steepest grade on the Washington State section of the Milwaukee Line. The Boylston Tunnel is 1973 feet long, with a slight curve at the west end. Be prepared with a flashlight and watch for horned owls in the rock cuts at both ends of the tunnel. Just east of the tunnel is a watering place for livestock and a meadow. From the Boylston Tunnel down to the Columbia River the average grade is 2 percent, compared with the 1.5 percent grade climbing from Rattlesnake Lake to the Snoqualmie Tunnel.

The U.S. Army condemned this property and uses it for military maneuvers, adding it to their huge Yakima Firing Center. They have destroyed the fragile railroad grade, which was built on sandy soil, with their heavy equipment and tanks. Be aware that they can close this section of trail whenever they deem necessary and that you may hear noises or see military personnel practicing cross-country driving. This spoils the ambiance that this section of the trail used to have. This is dry country, with no road access for 100 years, and the land probably is just as it was when the railroad built the line. Enjoy the downhill grade and look east for the first glimpses of the Columbia River.

A long steel railroad bridge crosses the Columbia River. This bridge has railway ties but no decking and is closed to public use. This is dangerous place to be, as evidenced by the boxcars at the bottom of the Columbia River that were blown off of this bridge by the strong winds. There are no services or facilities at the bridge, but the Washington State Parks and Recreation Commission operates the Wanapum Recreation Area 3 miles north along a country road, and there are services 6 miles north at Vantage. Note how the Columbia River has cut through the Saddle Mountains to the south.

This trail is very popular in the winter for cross-country skiing and other snow sports. For example, the Snow King Alaskan Malamute Fanciers hold their annual Freight Race on the trail in South Cle Elum each January. Most of the route generally is safe from avalanches, except where the snow sheds have been removed, and its level terrain makes it ideal for beginning cross-country skiers.

This trail was opened in 1984 from Easton 25 miles east to tunnel 47. This portion of the trail was named the John Wayne Pioneer Trail at the behest of the citizens' group that helped convince the legislature to acquire the entire right-of-way in 1981. In 1989 the Washington State Parks and Recreation Commission's ownership was extended to the Columbia River and in the future may include the rest of the Milwaukee Road Corridor all the way to Idaho.

44 Lower Yakima Pathway

Yakima County Parks and Recreation, City of Grandview Parks and Recreation, City of Sunnyside Parks and Recreation

Endpoints: Sunnyside to Prosser
Length: 14.0 miles
Surface: asphalt
Restrictions: none
Location: Sunnyside and Grandview, Yakima County
Latitude/longitude: N46° 18.75'/W119° 58.65'
Elevation: 722 feet at Sunnyside, 818 feet near Prosser

This trail is located on a railroad right-of-way next to a busy road. It provides a safe place for walking and bicycling and connects two small communities.

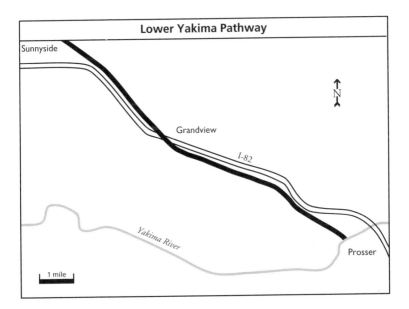

A sign of the dream to come

To get to the north trailhead in Sunnyside, follow I-82 to Sunnyside and take exit 67. Turn right onto Yakima Valley Highway and proceed to 16th Street. There is a park-and-ride lot at the start of the trail, which runs southeast between the highway and the railroad. To reach the middle trailhead in Grandview, take exit 73 (Stover Road) to Grandview and turn southeast toward town. You'll find a park-and-ride lot just south of Stover Road, where the rail-trail starts and heads north. To get to the south end, from I-82 take the Prosser exit and look for the southern end of the trail on the north side of the Yakima River bridge going into Prosser.

The only park along the route is the Lower Valley County Park, about 2 miles south of the Sunnyside trailhead. It has restrooms, water, and shade, all useful in this area. Nearby is a wine-tasting room for one of the many wineries in the Yakima Valley.

The trail follows an abandoned railroad line from Sunnyside to Grandview and then turns south to Prosser. It is generally near the freeway or highway but provides a safe alternative for all types of nonmotorized use.

This rail-trail is an example of an innovative project initiated by local citizens, who contributed much volunteer labor, and involving the cooperation of several agencies. The project was started by the General Federation of Women's Clubs of Lower Yakima Valley, and the trail is comanaged by the cities of Sunnyside, Grandview, and Prosser and Yakima County Parks. The land has been protected from development because of the railroad and highway easements. It now provides a nonmotorized route between two local communities along a very busy highway.

45 Milwaukee Road Corridor Trail

Department of Natural Resources

Endpoints: Idaho border to Columbia River
Length: 143.0 miles
Surface: loose ballast, gravel, and sand
Restrictions: use by permit only October to May; some portions closed
Original railroad: Chicago, Milwaukee, St. Paul, and Pacific Railroad
Location: Tekoa, Rosalia, Lind, Warden, Othello, and Beverly in Whitman, Adams, and Grant counties
Latitude/longitude: N47° 14.41'/W117° 2.40'
Elevation: 2686 feet at Idaho Border, 510 feet at Columbia River

Traveling this rail-trail is an adventure in which you can relive the experiences of the early pioneers. The land and the rail-trail are rugged, with many hidden treasures along the way. Unlike many rail-trails in western Washington, this trail provides tremendous views because there are no large stands of trees lining the route.

To get to the east end, take SR 27 to Tekoa and look for the high railroad bridge over town. Turn right on Lone Pine Road 0.25 mile

north of the railroad bridge and proceed up a long hill. Where the road takes a sharp right, turn left on a dirt road and go 100 feet to get to the trail. Access is also good at the only other towns along the route: Rosalia, Lind, and Warden. The west access is at Beverly, 6 miles south of the I-90 Vantage Bridge on SR 243. Turn into Beverly and head east and then north to the old railroad depot.

Because of the long distances between access points, this trail is most appropriate for equestrian or mountain bike use. However, people do walk the entire route.

The wildlife along the route is incredible. Be prepared to see many different birds, including hawks, owls, and terns. Also look for porcupines, deer, rabbits, coyotes, and rattlesnakes. In many places, the railroad right-of-way has preserved a strip of natural vegetation that is often the only wildlife habitat for miles around.

Grain elevators originally were built along the route because the railroad was the only way to get grain to markets. Now the grain elevators are the lighthouses in this dry sea; they mark old train stations, road intersections, and sometimes small communities. They are welcome sights to the weary traveler.

The trail begins at 2686 feet in the Palouse Hills at the Idaho border and ends at 510 feet on the Columbia River, passing through four different geographic areas. Starting on the south slopes of Tekoa Mountain, it passes through the Palouse Hills and the dry scablands around Rock Lake, across the barren Rattlesnake Plateau, and down the Lind Coulee to Crab Creek and the mighty Columbia River. The natural terrain changes throughout the trip. Pine trees in the eastern Palouse give way to rolling hills with no trees for miles until Malden, where there are pine trees at a lower elevation. From Malden the trail runs alongside Pine Creek, with lush marshes and green vegetation all the way to Rock Lake. Rock Lake has steep basalt cliffs and pine trees its entire length. Below Rock Lake the trail climbs gradually to a high plateau of scablands, scrub grass, and basalt cliffs. At Ralston the trail enters the Lind Coulee, with a dry creek bed and grasslands. The last section, from Othello to the Columbia, lies in a broad valley between two hillsides where there are sand dunes and small lakes.

Travel on this trail is serious business. There are very few sources of food or water along the route and significant distances between supplies. Be prepared to undo barbed-wire gates and replace them after passing through. The Department of Natural Resources has not

Crossing the high trestles above Rock Lake

developed the trail surface; it varies from hard-packed gravel to soft gravel to uneven large gravel that is hard on feet, hooves, and bike tires.

The towns along this route range from very small to unrecognizable. The only available food is at Tekoa, Rosalia, Lind, Warden, and Othello. Drinking water is available at the gas station in Malden, the church in Ewan, and the town park in Ralston. Other names on the accompanying map are of old railway stations that used to dot this route and were created to provide water stops for the big steam locomotives. Unfortunately, they no longer exist.

The trail is used every year by the John Wayne Pioneer Wagons and Riders group, which sponsors a wagon train. During the 1989 Washington State Centennial celebration, more than 500 people participated in a wagon train crossing Washington State on this trail.

This rail-trail is so long that the most useful way to describe it is by geographic zones.

PALOUSE
Idaho Border to Rosalia, 26 miles
The trail unofficially starts at Tekoa, near the Idaho border. (The trail actually begins at the Idaho border, 5.6 miles east of Tekoa, where it is accessible by a few county roads.) Tekoa is a small town tucked in the folds of the land. The Milwaukee Road, the common name for the

Chicago, Milwaukee, St. Paul, and Pacific Railroad, was built going east to west across Palouse, whereas the other railroads ran along the valley bottoms. Consequently, when the Milwaukee Road Corridor Trail passes through Tekoa, it is on a huge trestle over Slippery Gulch. The trestle is so prominent that it is used as the background for the town's business cards. The trestle is closed, so to get to the trail going west, go north on Highway 27 out of town and turn left at the first bridge over the creek onto Lone Pine Road. Climb to the top of the hill and turn left 100 feet along a farmer's dirt road to the rail-trail. The trestle's west approach is 1.3 miles east from this point.

The trail paints a swath of green across the Palouse Hills. These hills were formed by years of prevailing easterly winds blowing topsoil to this location, and they are now quite productive. The 100-foot right-of-way has not been farmed, but every other inch of land is covered with crops. In the summer this makes the trail a ribbon of green draped across the tops of the hills. The trail gradually drops in elevation alongside the hills and crosses into Rosalia on a beautiful concrete arch bridge. Rosalia is a little town with a grocery store and a wonderful park. Coming into town, there is a missing trestle. Get off of the trail and go downhill into town.

PINES
Rosalia to Ewan, 29 miles

The trail through Rosalia lies on a hillside and is not easily accessible. To regain the grade, go out of town to the north and take the first road (Gashouse Road) that crosses the creek to your left. Take the first dirt road to the right that climbs up to the right-of-way. Traveling north out of Rosalia, you will soon see the large, beautiful Rosalia cemetery on your left. Pine trees begin to line the trail as it follows Pine Creek heading west. The bridge over Pine Creek provides a nice view of a lowland field to the south rimmed with pine trees.

Malden used to be a main railroad town with many railroad maintenance facilities. Today it is a very quiet, small community with one gas station that has drinking water. The old railway station is still in place, although it has seen much better days.

The route from here to Ewan has one gap of private ownership necessitating a detour around Rock Lake. To go around this private property you must leave the grade at Kenova and turn south on Stephen Road and then right on SR 23 to Ewan. It is possible to go part way down the lake on the trail before you need to backtrack, and it is well worth it. This is one of the most picturesque parts of the entire trail.

If you continue to Rock Lake you will pass over a large steel girder bridge on a curve over Pine Creek. There are still two steel boxcars lying on their sides where they fell off the trestle just before the line was abandoned. Just around the curve is a view of the area known as Hole in the Ground, a narrow canyon about 300 feet below.

Rock Lake is a 7-mile-long lake with steep basalt cliffs on all sides. The railroad was carved along the edge of the lake about 300 feet above the water. Pass through several tunnels and over some very airy trestles, which make the view even more spectacular. When you come to a wheat combine buried in the dirt across the trail, you have reached the private property. At the southern end of Rock Lake the right-of-way is still 100 feet above the lake level and provides a spectacular view up the lake to the north. You can gain access to the south end by going north from Ewan on Rock Lake Road. Where the trestle used to pass over the road is a gate signed for the Milwaukee Road Corridor. Go through the gate and head north. Stop at the private property that is indicated by a dirt mound and barbed wire across the trail about 2 miles north.

SCABLANDS
Ewan to Warden, 72 miles

Ewan is a community with a few houses, a grain elevator, and no public services. The railroad right-of-way is private for 0.4 mile north and 0.7 mile south of town. To continue south, go south on Cherry Creek Road for 0.125 mile and turn west on Cottonwood Creek Road for about a mile. At the end of the road is a small trail going north toward Rock Creek Falls and the Milwaukee Road Corridor Trail.

This area is called scablands because it is trying to heal itself from the tremendous scouring that occurred when at least thirty separate ice dams broke in Montana 12,000 to 14,000 years ago and released incredible amounts of water. These are known as the Spokane or Bretz floods, and they flowed over lower eastern Washington from here to the present course of the Columbia River to the west. During the floods this land was under 800 feet of water and was scoured by all the rock debris, removing most of the soil.

This land has very few trees. It is so rocky that it cannot be farmed except in the creek bottoms. But you'll find real wildness and beauty in the shapes carved into the rocks and in looking out to the horizon and not seeing human intervention (except for the railway grade). The land is used as range for cattle, but because it is so marginal there are few cattle per acre. There may be more deer than cows. It is the home of many wild animals: deer, coyotes, horned owls in every rock cut, jackrabbits, hawks, mice, grasshoppers, and birds.

Going west from Ewan you will come to a small area known as Revere, where the trail crosses Revere Road. The land near the grain terminal is still private land, so just use the county road until 0.2 mile west of the grain terminal.

The dramatic nature of the scablands is exemplified at Cow Creek. The railroad built a huge steel trestle across this creek. It has been removed, thus creating a workout for trail users. The view to the valley floor 200 feet below is wonderful. Contented cows graze on the only green grass for miles. It is so quiet you can hear them low. This is rattlesnake country, so be careful, especially in rock cuts.

Unfortunately, although the Department of Natural Resources owns a 200-foot right-of-way across the valley floor, there is no safe way to get to it because of the rock cliffs. That's why the railroad built a trestle here. To bypass the missing Cow Creek trestle, at Marengo take the county road on the south side of the trail and take the first right northwest into Cow Creek. Take the next sharp left and then the next right, climbing out of the valley and up and across the grade in about 1 mile.

The town of Ralston has three houses, no services, and a little park with a public drinking faucet. The trail from here to Lind parallels the Lind–Ralston Road through continuous sagebrush and land that is gentler than that you have passed through.

Lind is a town with services: a laundromat, motel, cafe, and grocery. There used to be a large trestle across the Lind Coulee, but it was removed for the steel.

The next section is a long 24 miles down a very dry, flat sagebrush valley away from any roads. The trail is so remote that it is easy to imagine why pioneers kept going west.

At Warden the trail ends, and the next 36 miles are an active railroad. The best alternative route is via the main highway to Othello. From Othello, continue west 8 miles on Highway 26 and turn left (south) on Gillis Road (gravel), and you will intersect the trail in 23 miles.

CREEK MARSHES
Smyrna to Beverly, 16 miles

Now the trail is at a lower elevation (600 feet) and follows Crab Creek to the Columbia River. Much of the land to the north of the trail is federal or state wildlife habitat.

The station stops of Smyrna and Jericho were named for places in the Bible. There are still homes at Smyrna, and if you look carefully you will see the old schoolhouse. The only remnant of the former station at Jericho is a log building. Just several hundred feet north of the trail are three lakes that have excellent fishing and attract many fishing enthusiasts.

Beverly is a small community next to the Columbia River, but the only public service is a post office. The old Beverly railway station is still in good repair. The Columbia River Bridge is closed to public access, but it is amazing to see. Going west, the trail connects with Iron Horse State Park at the west side of the Columbia River Bridge.

This trail is operated by the Department of Natural Resources; permits must be obtained from trail manager James Munroe (telephone 509-925-6131). Be sure to ask for a key for the numerous gates.

This rail-trail comprises a significant portion of the Washington Cross-State Trail, and citizen support is needed to get it developed for easy and safe passage. The Milwaukee Road is an important part of the Washington Cross-State Trail.

46 Neppel Landing Trail

Moses Lake Parks and Recreation

Endpoints: North Alder Street to W Marina Drive
Length: 0.5 mile
Surface: concrete and asphalt
Restrictions: no horses
Original railroad: active Columbia Basin Railroad
Location: Moses Lake, Grant County
Latitude/longitude: N47° 7.94'/W119° 16.72'
Elevation: 1057 feet

This is a great place to stroll along the water near the downtown area of Moses Lake. The trail parallels an active spur railroad line,

Neppel Landing Trail

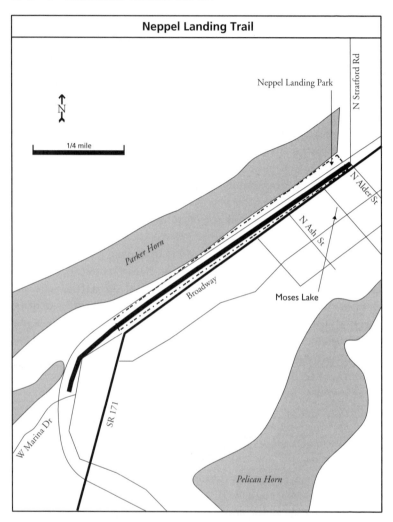

and the area has been grassed over, making a park. A small pier offers access to a good view of the lake.

To get to the trailhead, from I-90 take exit 179 north on Highway 171 (Broadway) to downtown Moses Lake. Turn left (west) on North Alder Street, and Neppel Landing Park is on the left. There is parking one block south of North Alder Street and west on North Ash Street behind the buildings. At the south end, the trail curves away from the tracks, crosses W Marina Drive, and becomes a wide sidewalk on the east side of the road for a few blocks.

Looking south along the path and tracks

This is a good example of a local neighborhood trail that provides public access to the waterfront and coexists with an active railroad.

47 Republic Rail-Trail

Republic Parks District

Endpoints: high school to fairgrounds
Length: 3.2 miles
Surface: gravel, sand, and asphalt
Restrictions: none; motorized vehicles permitted
Original railroad: Washington and Great Northern Railroad, built 1902
Location: Republic and Sanpoil, Ferry County
Latitude/longitude: N48° 38.65'/W118° 44.43'
Elevation: 2440 feet at Republic

This rail-trail is a local trail through the lower part of Republic out to the county fairgrounds east of town. It provides a good route connecting the city, high school, and fairgrounds. It also provides a safe alternative route to SR 20, a fairly busy highway.

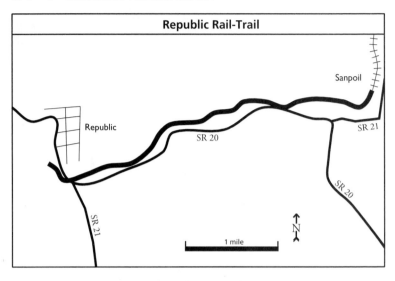

Republic is a city developed around the major mining claims in the area, some of which are still active and productive. Numerous railroad lines were built to the mines and up into the woods for logging. This line was the main line running north toward Curlew, where it connected with the Northern Pacific line.

To get to the west end of the trail, go to downtown Republic, turn west on Ninth Street, and go one block to Ripple Ball Field. The trail begins to the southeast below the steep bank below the main street. To get to the east end, go to the fairgrounds 3 miles east of town and look north across the highway for a public trail access to the rail-trail 400 feet north of the highway.

The rail-trail is built into the hillside above a marshy area that provides good wildlife viewing. It generally remains some distance from the main highway and goes through several deep cuts in the rock.

This rail-trail is open to motorized vehicles because they are very popular in this community. Off-road vehicles had used the route for years before the Republic Parks District bought it, and there is an established motorized route to bypass the state highway.

Plans are in the works to pave a portion of the trail. In the future, if the railroad line north is abandoned this rail-trail might continue to Curlew and perhaps to Canada. The road west from Curlew, West Kettle River Road, is located on the original Northern Pacific Railroad right-of-way.

A rock cut near San Poil

48 Spokane River Centennial Trail

Washington State Parks and Recreation Commission

Endpoints: Idaho to Nine Mile Dam
Length: 39.0 miles
Surface: paved
Restrictions: none
Original railroad: several
Location: Spokane, Spokane County
Latitude/longitude: N47° 39.69'/W117° 24.62'
Elevation: 1886 feet at Spokane, 2071 feet at Idaho border

This trail is a wonderful example of an urban trail leading into sub-urban and rural areas—in this case the Spokane area. It is also a link with the Centennial Trail in Idaho, which extends from the Idaho border east to Coeur d'Alene.

This trail originated because of the availability of an abandoned railroad line going east from the downtown core of Spokane. How-ever, the route does not follow the railroad right-of-way the entire way. Instead, it primarily follows the Spokane River. The newer segments developed to the west do not follow railroad grades at all, and there are still major gaps. But the development of this urban and suburban trail in the booming area of Spokane has become very popular with the people who live in this area.

This trail is suitable for different uses at different locations. The paved areas to the east make terrific bike routes. Farther east in the valley are less crowded areas that are more popular with equestrians.

The original trail began in downtown Spokane next to the Opera House. This area was redeveloped for the 1974 Spokane Expo, including a wonderful park on an island in the middle of the Spokane River. The trail lies close to the Spokane River and passes the convention center, large hotels, and office buildings.

Going east, the trail passes over the Don Kardong Bridge, named after a local runner who started the annual Bloomsday Road Race for runners, the second largest running race in the United States. The bridge is an old railway bridge that has been turned into an attractive viewpoint of the Spokane River. On the north bank across the river is the Museum of Native American Cultures and Gonzaga University.

The route runs alongside an active railroad and then follows Upriver Drive for several miles until it crosses the river to the south side on the Denny Ashlock Bridge. Here the river has lower banks, and the trail is sometimes right down in the floodplain along the water's edge.

The trail crosses the Spokane River several times going east,

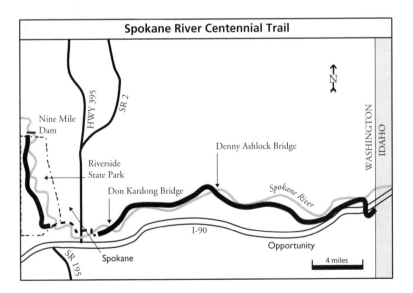

A crowd taking a walk along the Spokane River

taking advantage of the best land for a multiple-use trail. It is always close to the river and provides good access for nonmotorized boats.

The trail going west has a big gap between the downtown area and Riverside State Park. There is a good paved trail system through Riverside State Park, but it is not along a railroad grade.

This trail is a result of the efforts of a strong community committee specifically organized for its development. This organization produces an excellent brochure with a map, available at most outdoor stores. Major federal funding came through the assistance of Thomas Foley, former Speaker of the House of Representatives and a native of Spokane. In the future the trail will continue west of Nine Mile Dam, down the Spokane River another 12 miles to Little Falls Dam.

appendix

RAIL-TRAIL MANAGERS

Ben Burr Trail
City of Spokane Parks and Recreation
Taylor Bressler
N 809 Washington Street
Spokane, WA 99201-2233
509-625-6655
www.spokaneparks.org

Bill Chippman Palouse Pathway
Pullman Parks and Recreation
Larry Fetter
Director of Public Services
P.O. Box 249
Pullman, WA 99263
509-334-4555, ext. 224
www.ci.pullman.wa.us/td

Burke–Gilman Trail
City of Seattle SeaTrans Department
Peter Lagerwey
210 Municipal Building
600 Fourth Avenue
Seattle, WA 98104
206-684-8022
www.ci.seattle.wa.us/td

Burlington Rail-Trail
Skagit County Parks and Recreation
Loren Cavenaugh
219 S Skagit Street
Burlington, WA 98233
360-755-9649
www.skagitcounty.net

Cascade Trail
Skagit County Parks
Peter Mayer
315 S Third
Mount Vernon, WA 98273-3822
360-336-9414

Chehalis Western Trail
Thurston County Parks
Chuck Groth
2617A 12th Court SW
Olympia, WA 98502
360-786-5595
www.co.thurston.wa.us/Parks

Coal Creek Trail
King County Parks
Tom Eksten
2040 84th Avenue SE
Mercer Island, WA 98040-2222
206-296-7808
www.metrokc.gov/parks

Coal Mines Trail
City of Cle Elum
P.O. Box 451
Cle Elum, WA 98941
509-674-2262

Columbia Plateau Trail
Washington State Parks and Recreation Commission
Gary Viem
P.O. Box 157
Starbuck, WA 988359
509-646-9218
www.parks.wa.gov

Cowiche Canyon Trial
Cowiche Canyon Conservancy
P.O. Box 877
Yakima, WA 98907-0877
509-575-4124
www.cowichecanyon.com

Douglas Creek Trail
Bureau of Land Management
Jim Fisher
1133 N Western
Wenatchee, WA 98801
509-665-2100
www.or.blm.gov

Dungeness River Bridge Trail
Jefferson County Parks and Recreation
Nick Warden
P.O. Box 2070
Port Townsend, WA 98368
360-385-9160
www.co.jefferson.wa.us/publicworks/parksrec/default.htm

Duwamish Bikeway
City of Seattle SeaTrans Department
Peter Lagerwey
210 Municipal Building
600 Fourth Avenue
Seattle, WA 98104
206-684-8022
www.ci.seattle.wa.us/td

Foothills Trail
Pierce County Parks
Claudia Peters
9112 Lakewood Drive SW
Tacoma, WA 98499
253-798-4048
www.co.pierce.wa.us/abtus/ourorg/parks/trails.htm

Interurban Trail
Everett Parks and Recreation
Daryl Bertholet
802 East Mukilteo Avenue
Everett, WA 98203
425-257-8300
www.ci.everett.wa.us/EVERETT/parks

Iron Horse State Park
Washington State Parks and Recreation Commission
Keith Wersland
P.O. Box 26
Easton, WA 98925-0026
509-656-2586
www.parks.wa.gov

Issaquah Creek Trail
King County Parks
Tom Eksten
2040 84th Avenue SE
Mercer Island, WA 98040-2222
206-296-7808
www.metrokc.gov/parks

King County Interurban Trail
King County Parks
Tom Eksten
2040 84th Avenue SE
Mercer Island, WA 98040-2222
206-296-7808
www.metrokc.gov/parks

Lake Whatcom Trail
Whatcom County Parks and Recreation
Roger DeSpain
3373 Mount Baker Highway
Bellingham, WA 98226
360-733-2900
www.co.whatcom.wa.us/parks/trails/trails.htm

Lake Wilderness Trail
King County Parks
Tom Eksten
2040 84th Avenue SE
Mercer Island, WA 98040-2222
206-296-7808
www.metrokc.gov/parks

Larry Scott Memorial Trail
Jefferson County Parks and Recreation
Nick Warden
P.O. Box 2070
Port Townsend, WA 98368
360-385-9160
www.metrokc.gov/parks

Lower Yakima Pathway
Yakima County Parks and Recreation
Dave Veley
1000 Ahtanum Road
Union Gap, WA 98903-1202
509-574-2430
www.co.yakima.wa.us/pubworks/parks.htm

Milwaukee Road Corridor Trail
Department of Natural Resources
Jim Munroe, Milwaukee Corridor Specialist
715 E Bowers Road
Ellensburg, WA 98926
509-925-6131
www.wa.gov/dnr

Myrtle Edwards Park Trail
City of Seattle Engineering Department
Peter Lagerwey
210 Municipal Building
600 Fourth Avenue
Seattle, WA 98104
206-684-8022
www.cityofseattle.net/parks/parkpaces/Medwards.htm

Neppel Landing Trail
City of Moses Lake
Jerry Thaut
401 S Balsam
Moses Lake, WA 98837
509-766-9240
www.mlrec.com

Northwest Timber Trail
Department of Natural Resources
Jim Matthews
P.O. Box 68
Enumclaw, WA 98022-0068
360-825-1631
www.wa.gov/dnr

Old Robe Historic Trail
Snohomish County Parks and Recreation
Mark Krandel
9623 32nd Street NE
Everett, WA 98205
425-388-6600
www.co.snohomish.wa.us/parks

Port Angeles Urban Waterfront Trail
City of Port Angeles Parks and Recreation
Scott Brodhun, Director of Parks and Recreation
240 W Front
Port Angeles, WA 98362
206-457-0411, ext. 215
www.ci.portangeles.wa.us/menus/parks.htm

Preston Railroad Trail
Department of Natural Resources
Jim Matthews
P.O. Box 68
Enumclaw, WA 98022-0068
360-825-1631
www.wa.gov/dnr

Preston–Snoqualmie Trail
King County Parks
Tom Eksten
2040 84th Avenue SE
Mercer Island, WA 98040-2222
206-296-7808
www.metrokc.gov/parks

Railroad Bikeway
Bellingham Parks and Recreation
Leslie Bryson
3424 Meridian
Bellingham, WA 98225-1764
360-676-6985
www.cob.org/cobweb/parks/index.html

Raymond–South Bend Trail
City of Raymond
Rebecca Chaffee
230 Second Street
Raymond, WA 98577
360-942-3451

Republic Rail-Trail
City of Republic
Larry Beardslee
County Courthouse
Republic, WA 99166
509-775-5231

Seattle Waterfront Pathway
City of Seattle SeaTrans Department
Peter Lagerwey
210 Municipal Building
600 Fourth Avenue
Seattle, WA 98104
206-684-8022
www.ci.seattle.wa.us/td

Snohomish–Arlington Centennial Trail
Snohomish County Parks and Recreation
Mark Krandel
9623 32nd Street SE
Everett, WA 98205
425-388-6600
www.co.snohomish.wa.us/parks

Snoqualmie Centennial Corridor Trail
City of Snoqualmie
Jeff Mumma
P.O. Box 987
Snoqualmie, WA 98065-0987
425-888-5337
www.ci.snoqualmie.wa.us/index.html

Snoqualmie Valley Trail
King County Parks
Tom Eksten
2040 84th Avenue SE
Mercer Island, WA 98040-2222
206-296-7808
www.metrokc.gov/parks

South Bay Trail
Bellingham Parks and Recreation
Leslie Bryson
3424 Meridian
Bellingham, WA 98225-1764
360-676-6985
www.cob.org/cobweb/parks/index.html

South Ship Canal Trail
City of Seattle Engineering Department
Peter Lagerwey
210 Municipal Building
600 Fourth Avenue
Seattle, WA 98104
206-684-8022

Spokane River Centennial Trail
Washington State Parks and Recreation Commission
Jack Hartt
4427 N Aubry Lane White Parkway
Spokane, WA 99205
509-456-3964
www.parks.wa.gov

Spruce Railroad Trail
Olympic National Park Visitor Center
600 E Park Avenue
Port Angeles, WA 983662
360-452-0330
www.nps.gov/olym/home.htm

Sylvia Creek Forestry Trail
Washington State Parks and Recreation Commission
Dan Kincaid, Park Ranger
P.O. Box 701
Montesano, WA 98563
360-249-3621
www.parks.wa.gov

Upper Snoqualmie Valley Trail
King County Parks
Tom Eksten
2040 84th Avenue SE
Mercer Island, WA 98040-2222
206-296-7808
www.metrokc.gov/parks

Wallace Falls Railway Grade
Washington State Parks and Recreation Commission
P.O. Box 230
Gold Bar, WA 98251-0230
360-793-0420
www.parks.wa.gov

West Tiger Mountain Railroad Grade
Department of Natural Resources
Jim Matthews
P.O. Box 68
Enumclaw, WA 98022-0068
360-825-1631
www.wa.gov/dnr

Whatcom County Interurban Trail
Whatcom County Parks and Recreation
Roger DeSpain
3373 Mount Baker Highway
Bellingham, WA 98226
360-733-2900
www.co.whatcom.wa.us/parks/trails.htm

Woodard Bay Trail
Thurston County Parks
Chuck Growth
2617A 12th Court SW
Olympia, WA 98502
360-786-5595
www.co.thurston.wa.us/Parks

index

about the author

Fred Wert spent much of his youth accompanying his father on steam engine rides all over the Northwest. He is an active bicyclist, hiker, and mountaineer, and his outdoor activities and knowledge of railroads led him to explore rail-trails before many of them were actually developed. He was instrumental in developing the Washington State Chapter of the Rails-to-Trails Conservancy and served as their first state coordinator. He now works as a consultant on rail-trail development and has participated in developing many of the trails in this book. He serves on the board of the Washington Wildlife and Recreation Coalition and is the planning director for the Trans-Continental Trails Association and chair of the Pacific Regional Trails Coalition. Mr. Wert's company, Rail-Trail Planning Services, sponsors the Rail-Trail Resource Center on the World Wide Web at *www.rail-trail.org*. He can be reached at *fredwert@rail-trail.org*.

THE MOUNTAINEERS, founded in 1906, is a nonprofit outdoor activity and conservation club, whose mission is "to explore, study, preserve, and enjoy the natural beauty of the outdoors . . . . " Based in Seattle, Washington, the club is now the third-largest such organization in the United States, with 15,000 members and five branches throughout Washington State.

The Mountaineers sponsors both classes and year-round outdoor activities in the Pacific Northwest, which include hiking, mountain climbing, ski-touring, snowshoeing, bicycling, camping, kayaking and canoeing, nature study, sailing, and adventure travel. The club's conservation division supports environmental causes through educational activities, sponsoring legislation, and presenting informational programs. All club activities are led by skilled, experienced volunteers, who are dedicated to promoting safe and responsible enjoyment and preservation of the outdoors.

If you would like to participate in these organized outdoor activities or the club's programs, consider a membership in The Mountaineers. For information and an application, write or call The Mountaineers, Club Headquarters, 300 Third Avenue West, Seattle, WA 98119; 206-284-6310.

The Mountaineers Books, an active, nonprofit publishing program of the club, produces guidebooks, instructional texts, historical works, natural history guides, and works on environmental conservation. All books produced by The Mountaineers Books fulfill the club's mission.

Send or call for our catalog of more than 500 outdoor titles:

The Mountaineers Books
1001 SW Klickitat Way, Suite 201
Seattle, WA 98134
800-553-4453
mbooks@mountaineers.org
www.mountaineersbooks.org